Your Talking Pet

Ann Walker

Your Talking Pet

©1997 Ann Walker

ISBN 1 898307 87 3

ALL RIGHTS RESERVED

Cover design by Paul Mason

Published by:

Capall Bann Publishing
Freshfields
Chieveley
Berks
RG20 8TF

In memory of Cindy, died September 1st 1991

So many ears have cheerfully pricked,
So many tails have wagged for me,
So many tongues have lolled and licked
And deep brown eyes have brightly shone,
All telling a love I've taken for granted
Now one of these faithful hearts has gone,
Leaving a void, rich memories too;
Cindy, the Big Red Dog, has gone home.
May she meet in the Heavenly Hunting Ground
Old friends of us both, the loved and the known
And when my turn comes to cross the Styx
I shall look for the friendly tails to wag,
For the loving eye, and the ears to prick
Welcoming me, as their spirits greet mine.

Contents

Introduction

We call them pets, a somewhat condescending word for those animals we select to live in our homes and share our lives in a relationship often as close, or even closer, than that we have with our human family. Like the human members of our family, we sometimes live together without ever really understanding one another. The reason for this is all too obvious; it is not lack of affection but a breakdown in communication.

Relationships are about communication; and there are more ways of talking than verbal speech, this is often the least important (or effective) method of getting through as we know in our dealings with our own kind. We all find in moments of intense emotion that words are inadequate.

We are not always aware how much we use non-verbal methods of communication; a smile, a scowl, a touch of the hand, a shrug of the shoulders. All convey so much. Animals are observant and we can utilise this quality in our dealings with them.

My sister had a wonderful pony called Happy when she was a child. They had a very close relationship and she taught him a range of tricks. One of these was to answer simple yes/no questions by either shaking or nodding his head. She did this by using a little stick and tapping him on one part of the shoulder for *yes* and another part for *no*. She then discarded the stick and used her finger instead.

1

Finally, she did not touch him at all but merely moved her finger. By this slight signal, never observed by the human onlookers, Happy knew whether to shake or nod. Observers were invariably impressed by this display of what they considered human intelligence and understanding in a horse, but I think the *real* communication behind the facade was far more impressive. This is the sort of talk that makes for a good relationship, one that can give pleasure, satisfaction and deep happiness to both parties.

Ann Walker, Eaglehawk 1995.

Chapter One

Beginning To Understand

Everything, whether it is a book or a cathedral, has its first spark of life as a thought in the mind of its creator.

The idea for this book began to take shape early one morning when I was in that pleasantly relaxed Alpha state between sleeping and waking. Tara, the Siamese cat who shares my life, had just patted my cheek with one doe-soft paw, all claws sheathed. This is her customary signal to me to raise the bedclothes so that she can wriggle in beside me where she turns round so that our two heads are side by side on the pillow. Drowsily I murmured greetings and she replied with a satisfied purr; a comforting sound, guaranteed to keep me drowsy. This is our early morning ritual; only varied when the weather is too hot for her to get into bed when she sits on the pillow about two inches from my head instead. I know of no sound more conducive to a relaxed and meditative mind than the soft thrum of a contented cats purr close to one's ear.

I thought about my relationship with Tara, and the understanding that had grown up between us over the years. I often boast that she understands every word I say, but I doubt if she could say the same of me!

Siamese are the language teachers of the feline world, they not only talk louder and more than other cats, but also seem to have a larger vocal range. I have heard of people actually getting rid of their cat because it talked too much!

When Tara is loudly demanding her meals, I am reminded of a small boy who told me that his mother bred both Chinchillas and Siamese.

I like the Siamese best, except at tea time, he confided.

Why not at tea time? I asked.

He looked at me pityingly; how could I, who lived with a Siamese, ask such a patently foolish question?

Because they shout so loud when they want their tea, he explained patiently.

This particular morning, my thoughts wandered into the past. I remembered the many animal friends who had shared my life and given me companionship and comfort. When I realised how many of them had joined me through their volition rather than mine, at a time of personal hurt, loss or trauma (too many to be coincidental), I saw these animals we rather condescendingly consider our pets with quite a different perspective.

It was almost as if I had turned the telescope right round so that instead of my big human soul looking at all these little animal souls and helping them, I was suddenly the little soul *being* helped! The startling thought occurred to me that maybe I, along with most of the rest of the human race, had got it all wrong; we weren't superior at all, at best we were equal, at worst inferior, and that in fact *they*, the animals, are really *our* teachers.

A salutary thought indeed; and it didn't stop there but led to a whole train of thoughts about animals and our relationships one with another, what we were here for, and what they were here for and the whole vast network that is the web of life on planet Earth.

A lot depends on how you measure superiority. We may have bigger and better brains that have enabled us to develop remarkable technological skills; but what about our souls; and which will benefit us most in the final count-down? We were not always so superior anyway. Trillions of years ago when Man was just a rather naked ape battling it out with all the other creatures, it certainly was not a foregone conclusion that we would inherit the earth. What was the crucial factor that brought us to our point of power? It was probably touch and go between us and the elephants, we won by developing our hands; to do this effectively we had to become upright. The elephant chose to remain on all fours and develop his nose into a trunk, he did this efficiently, as we did our hands, but of course he only had one nose. Having become upright and discovered what we could do with our hands, we then concentrated on our brain, with this winning combination of hand and brain, we became the master animal, even over the mighty elephant.

It is brain power, not soul power, that has got us where we are today. If our spiritual development had kept pace with our intellectual advancement, we would not be in such danger of blowing our planet and ourselves, right out of existence.

Our big stumbling block in successful inter-species communication is our superiority complex. We are so conscious of being human *beings* (as a small child I thought we were human beans!) and many rungs up the evolutionary ladder. Whoever heard of a dog being, or a cat being, still less of a cow or sheep being? It is not so much the dumbness of animals but our sense of superiority that blocks effective communication. The fact that understanding between different animals is often so good, bears this out.

Dogs and cats, who, as Alice in Wonderland pointed out, have a diametrically opposite way of communicating, can live together in perfect harmony and great affection, quite obviously understanding each other perfectly. Yet we, out of our superiority, have coined the phrase dog and cat relationship to describe two people who cannot get on together.

Tara and Ashley (my loving, loyal, intelligent, but - oh, so clumsy Labrador cross) have a wonderful relationship and appear to have no difficulty whatsoever in understanding each other's language.

Ashley, who is quite prepared to defend Tara with her life from bullying by neighbourhood cats, is reduced to a quivering jelly at the first breath of thunder in the air. With every roll or rumble she runs round in circles, tries to squeeze her portly body into impossibly small safe places, or clamber onto a human lap. I have seen Tara, who is unperturbed by thunder (but extremely fond of her creature comforts) leave her warm spot by the heater to comfort Ashley at each clap of thunder, rubbing her face against her friend and making soft feline prrrts of reassurance and getting through to Ashley better than I ever can in the same circumstances.

Looking back down the vista of the years, I can see how very many of the important lessons were given by my animal friends. One of the first things I can remember at all is a lesson in sharing in which the family dog was as much my teacher as my mother was. Rowley, who was a sturdy Sealyham, small in stature but large in character, was part of the life and family I was born into. He was given to my parents as a wedding present three years before I was born and was so much their child that well-meaning relatives predicted doom and disaster when a baby arrived to threaten his security. Fortunately for us all, my parents ignored these warnings and, as they had believed he would, Rowley just accepted me as the new puppy in the family. On this particular day, I was chewing on a bone, a chicken drumstick, which my mother had given to me as a natural teething ring. I poked it at Rowley and probably thinking that I was offering it to him, he grabbed his end and held on - tight. The ensuing fracas, he growled and I howled, as we fought for the bone we each considered our own, brought Mother hurrying to the scene. She dealt with the situation by removing my fingers, and not, as I had fully expected, Rowley's teeth.

I was impressed. This dog was some person if he could convince my mother, at that point in my life the fount of all wisdom and authority, that he, not I (to whom, after all the bone had been given in the first place) had a greater claim.

Alas, I was a slow learner! A few years later, I was visiting a zoo with my parents, I had a brand new propelling pencil and I poked it through the bars of a cage at one of the monkey inmates who immediately snatched it. Within seconds he had dismantled it. Seeing my small treasure thus reduced to a pile of useless bits and pieces, I gave vent to my feelings. Any expectations I may have had that my father would dry my tears and somehow, miraculously, retrieve the bits and make my pencil whole again, were firmly dashed. Quite the reverse, I was delivered a stern lecture on my selfishness.

The poor monkey, my father pointed out, was incarcerated in a lamentably small cage with no toys and nothing but the endless procession of people past his cage to relieve the dreadful tedium of his life. The pencil, which he no doubt thought I was offering him as a gift, had afforded him a few moments at least of enjoyment and interest; surely, he asked, I would not grudge him such a small pleasure?

7

I stopped bawling, sniffed and looked at the monkey with new understanding. It looked back, for a moment our glance held; I felt a swift current of communion flow between us. This was just another child like myself! In that moment I felt it was indeed thanking me for the gift so unwillingly and ungraciously bestowed. I was touched by the compassion, felt so strongly by my father, which had caused his anger. Fleetingly, I understood, I cared, and I gave up my toy with good grace.

Of course, these two lessons in sharing, did not turn me into a generous and unselfish child overnight, nor did it ensure that I grew up into a generous and unselfish adult, but if nothing else, it gave me a sense of equality with, rather than a superiority over, the animals I met in daily life.

If it is true that we absorb most of the really important lessons in life before we even start school, then animals, in particular one diminutive dog called Mickey, was one of my most important teachers.

Poor Rowley died not too long after the bone incident and Mickey joined the family, or rather joined our branch of it to be correct. His mother, Dora, was a remarkable little dog, about one part toy poodle and three parts Yorkshire Terrier. She lived with my fathers brother and his family.

As an only child for the first six years of my life, I always thought of Mickey as a sibling rather than a family dog. I never thought of him as inferior, or less intelligent or important; and I am sure he didn't either. He was remarkably tolerant and would allow me to dress him in my dolls clothes, put him to bed in my dolls cot and even wheel him around in the dolls pram. During one unfortunate period when I planned to be a hairdresser when I grew up, he even allowed me to trim his beautiful silky fringe. My mother was very annoyed, as much with him for allowing me to do it as with me for doing it. I also respected him and knew that though he would allow me to share the big armchair with him, he would definitely *not* allow me to push him out of it and take it all for myself, another lesson in sharing. In the many years he lived with us he taught us all a great deal, about love, and friendship, and courage and communication.

One memorable occasion when my father was away from home for the night, my mother was roused by Mickey at about 2 am, not barking with his shrill small terrier yap, but standing on the bed patting her urgently with his paw. Somehow she got the message, climbed out of bed, threw a robe round her shoulders and followed him down the stairs. It was full moon and again, she told us afterwards, she seemed to be obeying Mickey, she did not put on any lights. Downstairs in the hallway, she could see the figure of a man outlined through the glass panel of the door. She and Mickey looked at one another, and in silent agreement, crept back up the stairs together. Both feeling that in this case, discretion was the better part of valour!

There are many interesting aspects to this little story. Neither Mickey nor my mother were quiet people. Each usually had plenty to say in their own way. It was equally uncharacteristic of my mother to meekly obey anyone, much less a small dog. In fact, she often wondered about this aspect of the story herself. Expressing more surprise that she had done what Mickey told her to do than the fact that she had understood exactly just what he was communicating to her.

The fact that Mickey woke her from her sleep probably accounted for this. She would be in a relaxed alpha state of consciousness, just the condition to be receptive to communication from another mind. A mind that must have gone into top gear when Mickey knew there was a stranger outside and with my father away, who was there but him, to watch for the safety of the helpless females in the house? This little incident also illustrated very clearly that although animals may not think in words, or communicate verbally, this does not mean that they do not think or know how to communicate.

Mickey had one special communication skill that is rare, but not unknown, in dogs. He smiled!

It is quite surprising that animals should even recognise a smile, let alone smile back, for baring the teeth and curling up the lip is often a sign of aggression in many animals including dogs, yet most do and some, like Mickey, even smile themselves. He did it to express pleasure, when we returned home after an outing, when he knew he was to be included in an outing, and when friends or other family members for whom he had a particular liking came to visit. Those favoured by Mickey's smiles were always pleased and flattered.

Though few dogs may do it themselves, most understand a smile from a human. I had to visit a local JP one day to get some documents signed, while he was doing it I smiled at his dog, a charming bitser who was sitting in front of me studying me with interest, immediately his ears relaxed into the smile position and his tail thumped on the carpet. In that momentary exchange, friendship had been offered and accepted, we had, in fact, communicated. An interesting little exercise in talking to an animal that can be done at any time and the pleasure found in making such contact will not pall, however many strange dogs smile back at you!

I have yet to meet a smiling cat (out of fiction) but then the Cheshire Cat was unique. That does not mean they do not watch our facial expressions just as carefully as dogs. The fact that they do is borne out by the undeniable fact that in a room full of people a cat will so often choose the lap of the one cat-hater in the room.

The explanation is quite simple; a total lack of understanding of each others body language, resulting in some very crossed wires!

The person who dislikes and is afraid of cats avoids looking at one directly, if their feeling is so strong that it amounts to a phobia, they may even close their eyes momentarily in horror. All this is the exact opposite to cat language. With them avoiding direct eye contact is a sign of deference, conciliation; with almost all animals, staring directly into their eyes is an act of deliberate aggression. Closing the eyes in a sort of slow blink is a cat equivalent to blowing a kiss. So the cat-hater, who thinks they are saying: "Keep away from me you frightful creature, I cannot even bear to look at you"! is actually saying, in cat talk I think you are a very nice, and slightly superior, being and I would like to be friends.

Naturally, the cat, receiving this message, jumps happily onto the cat-haters lap! Just occasionally, the long term effect of such monumental misunderstanding can be good. A few years ago, I was taking a fortnightly discussion group on *a course in miracles*. A fairly regular attendant was a student at a local College. Tara, who was always at the group, invariably chose her lap to sit on. At the end of the College year, the girl came to say good-bye to me. She thanked me for the evenings she had spent with us and added, "I've learned something really important coming along here." I listened eagerly expecting her to reveal some deep spiritual understanding she had gained from our regular reading and discussion sessions.

What a surprise when she said, "I shall never be afraid of cats again! I have been terrified of them all my life; but when Tara kept choosing my lap to sit on, I suddenly realised what a lovely little creature she is and that there is nothing in the world to be afraid of!" This little story also lends credence to the old adage that if you believe in something enough it eventually comes true! Tara, by repeatedly getting the message wrong and believing that she was liked, actually made this come about.

This happy outcome to a bad beginning is an exception. All too often, the cause of accidents and emotional hurt to one or both parties is the result of a complete failure to understand the language of the other. The greater blame for this lack of understanding is all too often with us humans. Acting from our superior position on the evolutionary ladder, we expect our dog or cat to learn to understand us, and we are not even prepared to meet it halfway.

Chapter Two

Learning To Listen

Communicating with our pets, or animal friends, means listening as well as talking. I realised just how few people were aware of this fact when my book *Talk With the Animals* was published and I did a series of radio, TV and newspaper interviews. Almost without exception the interviewers referred to the book as *Talk to the Animals* I repeatedly pointed out the correct title, explaining what a difference those two words made!

We *all* talk to our animals, even talk at them, it is only when we zip up and start listening that communication can even begin! Unfortunately, we are so hung up on speech that we find it hard to imagine any real communication without the use of words. Yet if we stop and think, we will realise that, even among our own kind, we actually do quite a lot of very important talking without words. How often have you caught someone's eye across a room and known that you are both thinking the same thing, maybe seeing humour in a situation that everyone else is taking seriously?

How often have you met your partner's eye and managed to convey, and/or receive the message that it is time you both left the party? In each case the message is very clearly given and received and yet not a word has passed between you. We can

Ashley has a very expressive face

communicate a wealth of feeling with body language; the warm hug, the simple pressure of a hand can express sympathy and understanding more fully than any amount of words. Some body language transcends differences of age, sex, race, even species, the open armed come to me I love you gesture will almost invariably get a response from both people and dogs, just try it! Most small children and dogs will run joyfully towards you when they see this warm loving gesture.

In our conversations with our pets, we almost invariably take the somewhat biased and unfair attitude that it is up to them to learn our language and we painstakingly teach them individual words, usually of command, and simple phrases. When they learn them and obey, we feel we have reached a satisfactory state of communication. The animal in the case may think quite otherwise! It is only when we actually stop talking and listen that we will have the faintest hope of getting even an inkling of what is going on in our small friend's mind. When I say listen, I really mean feel or listen with your heart and your eyes as well as your ears!

With animals, as well as people, you will inevitably find those with whom real communication is much easier than others. I often say that Ashley, my dog, has a very expressive face. Maybe she has and maybe she hasn't. What I really mean is that I personally, find her facial expressions easy to read so that I can see from her eyes, the set of her ears, the tilt of her head, much of what she is feeling and thinking, and I get the simple messages that she is endeavouring to get over to what must often seem my very thick understanding! For example: I remember one morning in particular, when each time I looked at her she gave me an expectant doggy smile and a little wag of her tail, each time she did this a picture flashed into my mind of one of our more regular walking places.

I have not the slightest doubt that she was suggesting a walk to me. When I said "Okay, we'll go!" She expressed the same excitement and pleasure that she does when I reach for her lead, before I actually did so.

The conversation of animals is usually very simple and direct, very much to the point and very much in the here and now. They do not lie or dissemble; if they like or dislike a person they usually make it quite clear. Over the years I have found it behoves me to take note of such feelings, for animals, like young children, go beyond the trappings and see right to the core of a person, and just know what they are really like. Some people think animals can see auras, this may well be so, certainly they seem to be able to see and recognise the true essence or soul of a person, while we, wiser and more sophisticated, cannot see beyond the clothes, the accent, the general facade which is often just the face they wish to present to the world and not their true self at all.

We know that when we act intuitively, when we follow our hunches and listen to our inner self, we are often in an Alpha brain wave pattern, animals and children are in this state much of the time which explains the belief that many people have in the special psychic powers of animals. Therefore it stands to reason that in order to really communicate with our animal friends, we too have to stop being so cerebral and left brain, operating in Beta and drop our own brain-wave pattern to Alpha so that we can communicate on the same level. This again is achieved by getting into a relaxed and meditative state. In such a frame of mind, we are receptive to hunches, listening to our inner intuitive voice or simply picking up messages from another mind.

Because we, alone of all the creatures, have developed speech and language to such a degree, we are apt to think that other beings have no means of communication, we may even fall into the trap of believing that because they do not speak, as we do, they do not think! This of course is patently absurd, any mother knows that long before her baby can speak, he is thinking and communicating. In actual fact, thought is far quicker than speech; we can think something in about a tenth of the time, or less, that it takes us to verbally explain it. Putting thoughts into words can considerably slow down, not speed up, communication. Whenever we try to develop any of our psychic faculties, and talking with our animal friends is no exception, we come up against two rather controversial ideas. On the one hand, in order to learn anything, it is necessary to concentrate and work on it, on the other hand, most psychic flashes seem to come to us when we are in a truly relaxed frame of mind and *not* trying to make anything happen! So - given this, how *do* we attempt a worthwhile communication with our animal friends?

I believe that animals think visually. That is, they see pictures in their mind, many humans also think like this and it is these people who are often very successful animal trainers because they are thinking like their pupils. Put very simply, in order to teach an animal something, you must first have in your own mind, a very clear picture of just what you wish it to do. If you can hold that picture there, then the animal may pick it up from your mind and see it in its own mind and thus be able to do what is required.

This, of course, is a two-way thing, I am quite sure that when a cat wants a drink of milk, it has a very clear picture in its mind of you, its person, getting the carton of milk from the fridge and obediently pouring it into its dish, this is often reinforced by body or even verbal language, the cat sitting at the fridge door, the demanding yowl, just as your commands have verbal and body language to supplement the clear picture in your mind when you ask an animal to do something.

There is nothing mysterious or rare in communicating with animals, we all do it all the time if we have any sort of animal companion. By becoming more aware of the process and

Sheba asking for a drink of milk

working on it, we can immeasurably improve the quality of our relationship; not only for ourselves, but for our animals too.

I often think how very stupid we must seem to our dogs and cats at times when we fail to get some message they are doing their best to get across to us. Ashley and Tara used to accompany me each day to my bookshop. On one occasion, I did the unthinkable and forgot to bring Tara home! Ashley kept making strange yawny noises at me from the back seat, I was half-way home before the ghastly thought hit me, I had forgotten Tara! I turned round at once and of course there she was, in her travelling case, waiting for me. Most unfairly I said to poor Ashley Why didnt you tell me I had forgotten her? (Being typically human, I had to find someone to blame!) I shall never forget the expression on her face, no words could have said more clearly; But I *did* tell you - you would not listen! That, of course, is the crux of most of our communication with animals; they tell us and we don't listen.

In order to get the message we must learn to be receivers as well as senders. This is often the hardest part of all, you may find it helps to visualise a white screen in your mind, when you wish to send a message you project onto the screen in your mind, the picture you wish the animal to pick up. Try and hold the picture there, uncluttered with extraneous bits and pieces that might also be picked up and thus confuse the issue. When you wish to receive, try and hold the screen quite blank and wait for a picture to be projected onto it. You may well find the latter far harder to do.

We are so used to words that most of the time we have to translate the message we get from our animal friends into our own language so that we say to ourselves; the cat wants a drink of milk or the dog wants to go for a walk, this does not mean, as one radio interviewer once tried to get me to say, that all animals speak English!

Another point to remember when we are working hard at this communication business is that animals have free will and they may not always want to talk to you! I well remember one occasion when I was practising on Matilda, one of my favourite cats who is usually very communicative so I practice on her a lot. This particular time however, even though I had worked hard getting myself into a suitably meditative frame of mind, getting the screen in my mind clear etc., In fact doing all the things I tell other people to do, there was no response from Matilda whose plump little black and white body was firmly seated on the floor near me with her back resolutely towards me. Suddenly, flashing into my head with a sharpness and clarity I could not ignore, came the message "Oh, Shut up! I dont *want* to talk to you!" In this case my mind had to translate the thought into words to be sure I received it and understood.

Animals do, of course, learn a great deal of our language, particularly if each time we give a certain command or use a phrase or word, we have the picture in our mind to match it. We can, and usually do, learn something of their vocal language. The sensitive dog owner will be aware of the many different barks their dog makes, the significance of each, and will know by the tone whether it is a stranger or a friend at the door. There can be few people unable to recognise the threat in a dogs growl or a cat's angry hiss. We are aware of these because our safety depends on it.

Developing this awareness so that we can enlarge and enhance the whole range of our communication with our dog or our cat, can be so rewarding that it can be likened to a door opening and revealing a whole new dimension to life itself.

Chapter Three

Who Teaches Who?

An ability to understand animals is an ability found in the spiritual greats of most cultures. Hiawatha learned every creature's language and secrets, St Francis regularly talked and listened to the birds and animals. He referred to everything as brother or sister. St Martin de Porres, the South American saint was also known for his love for animals that took the very practical form of caring for the sick and needy, he founded what was probably the first animal hospital in the world in the 16th century.

The Buddha too was known for his affinity with animals, and when he went into the forest they protected him and brought him food. Nearer to our own time, Ghandi loved, understood and cared for animals to the extent of making an important visitor wait while he tended a sick goat. Matthew Fox, one of today's great spiritual teachers, who has written many books on what he calls Creation Spirituality refers to his dog in his book *Original Blessings* as his Spiritual Director. A *Course In Miracles*, which is all about love and forgiveness, tells us that A Teacher of God is anyone who, at any point in time, does not see his own interests as apart from anothers.

By that criteria there can be few beings more qualified to be Teachers of God than the average dog who usually knows, and practices, more about love and forgiveness than you or I can hope to learn in a lifetime!

Most dogs understand all about loving unconditionally, something we humans often find so hard. When a dog loves, he does not ask his beloved to change in any way but accepts the person just as they are, never trying to make them into the person he thinks they should be. How many of us can truly say that we can love like that? For most of us the hoary old joke about the brides vow being Aisle Altar Hymn is all too true!

The dog does not even make it a condition of his love that he is loved in return. All too often, we not only give our love on condition that the beloved comes up to scratch and is the sort of person we want, but also that they should return our love in full measure. Failure to do either, and, feeling hurt and cheated, we withdraw our love. Psychologists tell us that around eighteen months of age we all become aware that the love of our parents cannot just be taken for granted but is conditional on us being good and pleasing them, how sad! No wonder that for so many children, the family dog is such an important person in their lives, instinctively they know that *he* will love them, no matter what.

A *Course In Miracles* defines forgiveness as forgiving your brother for what he did not do to you. In other words, the slight or whatever, simply did not happen, there is nothing to mar your relationship, quite different from the conscious superiority of the bestower of forgiveness! This is how our dogs forgive us for our grumpiness, carelessness and thoughtlessness, even for deliberate unkindness.

Animals can teach us something about the value of living in the here and now. For them this moment is all important; we humans lose so many of the precious moments of life by our determination to re-live the past or project ourselves into the future. All we really have is *now*, the past has gone, the future may never come. Dogs have such a wonderful ability to enjoy their now, and it takes so little to make them happy; a smile, a gentle touch, a kind word. A small gift of time and attention to do something he enjoys, a ride in the car, a ten minute walk in the bush, and he is ecstatic. If we could learn to be so undemanding, how much better might our relationships be?

Loving as they do so uncritically, dogs are great boosters to our self esteem; who *could* feel unlovable when they are the recipient of a dog's devotion?

Cats also have much to teach us, more complicated than dogs, yet no less loving and caring in their own unique way. There is one thing a cat will never do, that is flatter! Quite the reverse, they often seem to go out of their way *not* to let you know they think you important! Many times I have returned home from an outing to catch a glimpse of Tara, my little Siamese cat friend, watching for me through a window or hiding under a bush by the drive gate. By the time I have garaged the car and located my door key, she is sitting somewhere else altogether, her whole attitude one of studied indifference, just in case I might imagine that my comings and goings are of the least concern to her!

Cats can teach us a great deal, they can live perfectly in the moment, yet they are philosophers with endless wisdom and patience and they know how to extract the very best out of any situation they happen to find themselves in. They have mastered the arts of meditation and relaxation to perfection. If you live with a cat, there is certainly no need to go for relaxation classes; simply watch, and copy, your small feline friend who knows far better than most humans, just how to relax every part and muscle of her graceful little body. As for meditation, who can doubt that the perfectly relaxed cat with

Sheba meditating

the semi-closed dreamy slits of eyes is not deep in meditation. It is no doubt because she spends so much time meditating that the alert and wakeful cat is so very much alive and why cats show the effects of old age less than any other living creature.

So - who needs a Guru if they share their life with both a cat and a dog? Together they will keep a person sane and thoroughly balanced; with a healthy self-esteem that is neither low or inflated. They will teach patience and tolerance, love and forgiveness, satisfaction with our lot in life, and by living together in harmony (two creatures that we like to consider natural enemies) they show us the way to harmony in our own personal relationships with our own kind.

Our pets are also our teachers and they may have more influence than we imagine. We think we select our pets, but looking back over the many who have shared my life with me, I realise how often it was the other way round, *they* selected *me*; and quite often when I did do the choosing it did not seem to work out. I had just finished with boarding school for good and come home to live when I saw Piper in a pet shop window. A Golden Cocker Spaniel puppy just 7 weeks old, he radiated chocolate box charm. He looked at me with the brightest of shoe button eyes, tilted his head and I swear said "Buy me!".

Years later, when my own daughter was about the same age, she came home one day with a kitten she had bought in a pet shop. I asked her why she had bought it as we had a full complement of cats in the family at the time.

"She looked at me and said Buy me! - so I did!" She told me. However all that was in the future; on that long ago summer day, I had, I thought, a tough job ahead, persuading my mother that we really could not leave town without the pup in the window! As it turned out, the hard bit was getting her to the Pet Shop, once there my job was done. I guess the pup summed up the situation pretty quickly; *he* knew just who he had to convince. In the blink of an eye, it seemed, a cheque had been written, papers collected and we were walking out of the shop with one fat ecstatic pup wriggling in my arms and gleefully licking my face. He was my dog for about as long as it took us to drive home, then he was my fathers dog. The choice was entirely Pipers, to give Dad his due, he never did anything to win his affection, he studiously ignored him (or tried to), so much so that I was always drawing his attention. "Isn't he gorgeous?" I would say. "Isn't he clever? Don't you think he is lovely?" and so on. To which Dad always replied, "Yes. but he's *your* dog!".

He remained my dog, technically, through all the babyhood traumas; the first nights he howled through, the puddles on the floor, the chewed slippers, etc. Throughout that summer he remained ostensibly mine, I trained him to lead, took him walks and taught him to obey simple commands. Then Autumn came and one day Dad took out his gun. Inevitably, I lost out to heredity and the hunting partnership of man and dog forged over many generations.

He and I remained good friends, just as he was good friends with everyone else in the family, but it was to my father he gave his devotion.

How interesting it would be if, just for one day, we could really see ourselves through the eyes of our dog or cat. It would, I think, be a very salutary experience and at the end of the day, we would probably have to reverse our ideas about dumb animals, or at any rate, just which one of us is the dumb one! At no time do we display our stupidity and innate lack of understanding of animals, as when we devise so called intelligence or I.Q. tests. Real intelligence can only be assessed by daily observance, it is the things they do when they are *not* being tested, that show brains.

Over the years I have noticed that animals who use their feet as we use our hands are often the bright ones. When I was a child I had a pony who would hold one end of a carrot down with her hoof so that she could break a piece off the other end with her teeth. She got an awful lot of carrots because I loved showing off this skill of hers to visitors!

My most intelligent cats over the years have all used their paws very deftly. Tara can open cupboards and take lids of saucepans and other containers, and does so with annoying regularity to help herself to the contents. Cats have very soft paws with quite flexible joints and of course the sharp claws that they can extend or retract at will, are useful to hook things open. Dogs, with their much stiffer and more clumsy paws, can also use them quite effectively. We have all seen our dogs pawing at their blankets and beds to get them just so. Ashley uses her paws most efficiently if given an empty ice-cream or yoghurt container to lick out. I have seen her not only put a paw inside it to hold it still but actually hold a carton steady with a paw each side of it.

Almost all dogs learn to knock or scratch at doors to gain admittance and some cats are clever enough to jump up and open doors with latches. I have even known one cat who could open doors with knobs, he actually grasped the idea of holding and turning. Piper, the Cocker Spaniel who beguiled me into buying him only to become my father's dog, learned to scratch a door in such a way that it really did sound more like someone knocking, a skill that caused me acute embarrassment once.

It was a dark winter evening and Piper had asked to go out, shortly afterwards I heard him (or I thought I did) at the door. Reluctantly, I left the warm fire to let him in. I opened the door and nothing happened.

Normally he hurtled in as soon as the door opened, tail wagging his thanks he would hurry to his place on the hearth. I waited, nothing happened except that I was getting chilly.

"Come on in, you damn fool!" I snapped. I was answered by a discreet cough. Somewhat taken aback I pulled the door wider open to reveal an anxious looking little man I had never seen before obediently stepping forward. The result of our simultaneous action was that we met in the light thrown from the hall just about eye-ball to eye-ball.

"Oh", I spluttered, "I thought you were the dog!". An explanation that, as the dog in question seemed to have vanished into the night, did not really seem to improve matters. He turned out to be canvassing on behalf of the political party my parents did not support. I was told to be more careful in future who I commanded to enter.

We humans are assiduous trainers of animals. We teach them verbal commands and expect them to obey, and when they do we say the are well trained, or well schooled, and praise their intelligence. One exception to this is the domestic cat, who, as a rule, is far too intelligent to learn our commands, or to admit that she has learned them. Most cat lovers will admit that any training that has been done has been of them, by their cat.

We have certainly come a long way in our thinking and our whole attitude to animals since Descartes, the philosopher who taught that animals were mere things, incapable of thought. Today, most of us know differently, and there are College courses that teach not just animal behaviour but about our relationship with the animal world. We are slowly coming round to the understanding of the true wholeness of life. What effects one, effects all, and the animals themselves are helping to teach us this lesson.

In today's urban, mechanical and industrialised society, horses are the great healers and teachers. In direct ratio to the horse becoming less important in our working lives, it has become more important in our leisure. For many people it is the horse which takes them directly into the great outdoors, the natural world. The close relationship with a horse that anyone who rides one must have, is a complete revelation to many people learning to ride. Until then, a horse was a bicycle with legs instead of wheels and they are genuinely amazed to discover a creature with a distinct personality of its own, with likes and dislikes, fears and phobias, in fact quite like themselves. Anything but an automaton. There is, of course, nothing like a wise old horse to teach a green rider, a fact that was borne out to me over and over in the years when I was teaching people to ride. Of course, to say that all horses are kind hearted saints would be as patently absurd as it would be to say the same of all people.

The horse usually know far more about the rider and his or her capabilities (or lack of them) than the rider does about the horse. Inevitably, there are some horses who take advantage of an inexperienced or unskilled rider and do more or less as they please, there are also kind and caring ones who take care of such passengers.

I once bought a very wise old mare in a horse sale, Goldie was a palomino who must have been quite lovely in her youth. I bought her because I was sorry for her. No, sorry is not the right word to convey the black wave of utter misery that engulfed her. As I stood and looked at her it was almost as if she were begging me to *do* something to rescue her, she stood with drooping head, a bag of bones, her unkempt coat was crawling with lice. Not the sort of horse I wanted at all! Yet, I found myself bidding for her. Back home I de-loused her, de-wormed her, put a warm rug on her and put her in a good pasture with a couple of feeds a day.

A month later the transformation was astonishing. She was still old, youth once lost can never be recaptured, but her coat now shone like a new copper coin, her head was held high, all trace of depression gone and her intelligent eyes shone with new life. We began to ride her and found a wonderfully well educated pony who responded willingly and happily to the requests of her rider. She was too good to do nothing but we did not really need her so I put an advertisement in the local paper with a silent prayer that the right person would buy her. A very nice couple with a daughter of around 11 or 12 duly turned up to look at her.

They explained to me that they wanted a safe reliable pony for their daughter who, though she had a pony was still very much a beginner. The one she already had was so lazy that he could scarcely be persuaded to move and she was therefore making little or no progress as a rider. I explained that Goldie was extremely well trained and did not require vigorous kicking to make her move. The child mounted and rammed her heels into the old mares sides. Two seconds later Goldie had deposited her neatly on the ground and was looking at her in a way which said quite plainly; You dont need to do that to me! That, I thought, was the end of that, but the father turned to me.

"I'll have her!" He said. "You expressly said; don't kick her hard and she took no notice, but that pony dealt with her perfectly. She will teach her to ride all right". So off Goldie went, to teach yet another, in what I am sure must have been a long succession of children, to ride. The story had a nice little sequel. Several years later, I answered an advertisement for a saddle. I bought it, and when I wrote out the cheque and handed it to the woman who was selling it, her face broke into a wide smile.

"I thought I recognised you!", she exclaimed. "We bought Goldie from you. She was wonderful, taught our daughter to ride and then went to some friends of ours and taught their daughter, they still have her, but she lives in honourable retirement now".

How glad I was in that moment that I had once listened to the silent plea from a down and out old horse and bought her, against all common sense.

Chapter Four

Tails Tell Tales

The tails of most animals are much more than appendages, ornamental or otherwise, at the end of their bodies. The tail, as well as being useful to aid balance, keep off flies etc., is a very valuable means of communication. Most of us are well aware that dogs wag their tails to show pleasure, some of us, if we have read *Alice in Wonderland*, also know that cats do so when they are angry; but this is only the tip of the iceberg as far as tail talk goes.

Horses high tail to show high spirits and swish their tails in anger; donkeys twitch their tails to show impatience, a twitching that grows almost to a thrashing when they are really angry. The cats and dogs we live with in our homes, have a whole range of semaphored messages they can convey with their tails, a sort of sign language that is very easy to read for anyone prepared to pay a little attention.

It is really quite amazing that cats and dogs can get on together, as their language is so often diametrically opposite, it is surprising they do not live in a constant state of crossed wires. Yet, dogs and cats sharing the same home can, and often do, form very close relationships and live together in perfect harmony, and, apparently perfect understanding.

Tail language is one example of the difference, dogs wag their tails when pleased or happy, cats wag their tails when cross or angry, a movement that can vary from a twitching of the tip to a wholesale swishing of the entire tail.

A stiff perpendicular tail in a dog means, if not actually aggression, then certainly a this is my patch, 'I'm cock of the walk' attitude. Cats on the other hand, raise their tails to the perpendicular, like a little obelisk, as a form of greeting for those for whom they cherish an affection.

A drooping tail in a cat merely shows it is relaxed, a drooping tail in a dog shows depression, actually tucked between its hind legs shows defeat, subjection. We use the expression; with his tail between his legs to describe a person who has suffered some set-back, humiliation or knock in some way.

If we could learn to recognise the messages being given by tails, there would be far fewer misunderstandings between people and animals, some of which may be quite minor, others resulting in someone getting hurt.

Many people who have cats, and who claim to be cat lovers, also seem to have almost permanently scratched arms and hands. These scratches show a communication block somewhere in the relationship, and you can be one hundred per cent certain that this is with the human either not seeing, not understanding, or simply ignoring, the messages being given by the cat.

A twitching tail from a dozing curled up cat means; Back off! Dont invade my space - leave me alone - touch me at your peril. If you stroke a curled up cat with a twitching tail, its first reaction may be simply to curl into a tighter ball, this is because most cats are basically kind hearted and after all, humans can't help being so dumb! But if you continue stroking it, or (in the cats view) pestering it, sooner or later,

Cats and dogs can live together in harmony

depending on the length of this particular cats fuse, it will retaliate by scratching.

On a cold winter's evening when Tara is curled on her favourite chair by the heat, I have only to say the word bed for the end of her tail to start twitching, almost, it seems, of its own volition. This is not the time for idle chit-chat, I simply scoop her up firmly, another three or four inches of tail now waving quite vigorously, and carry her to bed.

If small children were taught both to understand the language of the family pets, and also to respect their wishes and feelings, there would be far fewer tears and more smiles all round. The twitching tail is nearly always the first warning, the back off signal. Failure to take note and act accordingly and twitching becomes angry thrashing.

Cats can also blow up their tails when really angry and/or scared. Even the long, skinny, rat-like tail of a Siamese can be blown up with each hair standing out at right angles to the tail itself so that it resembles a bottlebrush. A cat whose tail looks like this is fully charged in fight or flight mode and liable to do either at a second's notice.

A cat in a thoroughly frivolous frame of mind, will often use its tail as a toy, idly waving it and then pouncing on it. Kittens, when other toys are in short supply, will spend hours playing with their own tails. Mother cats often obligingly swish their tails for their small kittens to pounce on, one occasion when the tail is not wagged in anger, but is being used to give a first lesson in chasing a moving object.

It is noteworthy that Manx cats, a tail-less breed, develop a sort of chatter to use in moments of stress or emotion, obviously compensation for having no tail to use to express their feelings.

Tara has heard the word ɸbadɸ. In a few moments her tail will swish in anger

I remember one very dramatic tale of tails from my childhood, in retrospect quite amusing though at the time it seemed quite horrific.

Two neighbouring dogs, working Collies and fairly evenly matched, neither of them ours, decided for some reason, to have a fight in our back yard. My mother, a firm believer in action, urged my father to *do* something! She had already tried pepper, which had no effect on the dogs but brought on one of her famous sneezing fits.

She then rushed for a bucket of water, and while getting it, managed to let our own diminutive little part Yorkie, Mickey, out of the house, possibly.because she did not see him due to the pepper induced tears and sneezing. This may also have been why she missed the dogs entirely and threw the bucket of water over my father!

Mickey meanwhile, had hurled himself into the epicentre of the fracas and was hanging on valiantly to the ruff of one of the dogs. Whether it was the unexpected cold douche, or the sight of Mickey in the middle of the mayhem, I dont know, but something galvanised my father into sudden, and very effective, action. He grabbed one of the dogs by the tail, by accident or design, it was the one Mickey was attached to, and swung it round in circles. The effect on the other dog was remarkable, tail clapped in to signify its utter submission and admission of defeat, it slunk out of the yard as fast as it could.

My father gradually slowed down his swinging, he had built up such a momentum he could not stop suddenly, and let go the tail of the second dog. It staggered a bit when its feet hit terra firma, shook itself, threw my father a look of mingled fear and respect before, also with tail well and truly half mast, it followed its adversary out of the yard. Mickey shook himself, sneezed and grinned at us all, his little rudder wagging at full speed before following my father back into the

37

house, obviously quite satisfied that he (maybe with a little help from my father) had dealt with the situation very well indeed.

My father always told this story whenever the subject of fighting dogs came up, concluding with the firm assertion that this was the only possible way to stop a dog fight. I do not remember anyone ever having the temerity to ask what one did if both dogs had docked tails! If nothing else, this story clearly illustrates that there are more uses than communication for a tail.

We humans as a species, do some horrific and barbaric things to animals, not the least is cutting off their tails. For generations we did it to horses. Having no tail was supposed to make the back end, the hindquarters, look more powerful, so all horses used for draught work were docked as foals. My father, much ahead of his time, considered it cruel and barbaric as well as being disfiguring. None of the horses he bred had their tails docked; our Shires with their long flowing tails were quite unique. Now it is illegal in many parts of the world to dock horses' tails. The reasons given for the practice were that it enhanced the look of strength and power and that long tails got in the way of harness and reins.

No such practical reason can be given to defend the practice of docking dogs tails. It is done for fashion, certain breeds *always* have docked tails because we, as humans, have decided they look better that way. What arrogance!

Enlightenment comes slowly, but I have seen a few Jack Russell Terriers and even the occasional Cocker Spaniel with their tails left as Mother Nature made them. To me they appear more balanced in appearance and therefore more attractive; I hope many others will agree with me!

There is one breed of cat that is actually born without a tail; the Manx cat. But not everybody realises that a cat can be a pure Manx, as far as pedigree goes, and still have a tail.

The gene for no tail in Manx cats carries with it the potential to be lethal. Manx kittens can be born not only tailless, but hopelessly deformed or even dead.

A true Manx is not just a cat without a tail, it actually has a slight depression at the end of the spine where the tail would be if it had one, it also has an odd sort of double coat and hind legs that are longer than the front ones.

This has given it the nickname bunny cat and also gave rise to the bizarre legend that the first Manx was the result of a cross between a cat and a hare!

A litter of Manx kittens can contain rumpies, the true Manx, stumpies (with a short tail) and tailed cats. Consistent mating of rumpy to rumpy results in an over abundance of the dangerous tailless gene and usually means that the majority of kittens born will be either dead or too deformed to live a normal life.

Manx cats are often more clumsy than other cats when climbing or balancing. This is because they have no tail to aid their balance; just as the high wire artist needs a balancing pole to help keep him or her aloft.

Without this important adjunct to communication, Manx cats have to look for something else with which to express their feelings. Like us, who are also tailless, they use the voice. Manx cats, particularly rumpies, develop a strange kind of chattering which they resort to in moments of emotion or stress; occasions when other cats would use their tails to express their feelings.

Chapter Five

Man's Best Friend

The relationship between Man and Dog goes back at least 10,000 years and is based on the fact that each recognised the other as a potential helper in the all important business of hunting to stay alive. It probably began when the first man threw a bone to the first dog hanging around his fire.

There is a delightful legendary story of how this enduring relationship originated. When God first created the world and all the creatures in it a chasm opened up between Man and all the other living beings. The dog, seeing this and realising that he was about to be separated from Man forever, leaped across just in time, before the chasm was too wide, and has stayed by Man's side ever since.

A charming story, and one that gives the dog all the initiative in laying the foundation for the thousands of years of close relationship between the two species that has followed. The truth of the matter is that in many ways the innate nature of both Man and Dog is so similar that we start off from a point of natural affinity. We both like to live in packs with a leader. We are both, by nature, hunters and in those early days, there can have been little difference between cave man's dwelling and the cave or lair the dog chose to live in.

The dog, even though he did not succeed in actually mastering fire as the man did, soon learned to appreciate its special qualities of warmth and comfort. He also learned to overcome his fear of Mans fire and thus avail himself both of its comfort, and also of its deterrent qualities to other wild creatures, so much so that he was prepared to defend Man, his lair and his fire.

It was a short step from this to actually helping Man in the hunt in fair exchange for a place by the fire and a share of the meat. No doubt it was not long before dog families were living with human families, and while the males were off hunting, the females stayed home to rear and care for the young. The man would know that his woman was a good deal safer if a dog or so was left back at the cave to protect her.

So Man and Dog developed and evolved together, for the most part living together in harmony, providing of course that the dog was fully aware just who was pack leader, or top dog, in this arrangement!

The Lapps have a very similar legend explaining the close association between Man and Dog. The dog, they say, first allied himself with the Wolf against Man, then he realised that he would be better off if he swapped sides so he threw in his lot with Man. When he did so he lost the power of speech but retained the ability to understand it and added to this the power to read Mans thoughts.

Can our dogs read our thoughts? Most people would say yes and also that at times, they seem to understand a great deal of our spoken language.

Someone who had recently been through a session with a hypnotist and had gone back to his early days; reliving being quite a young baby, told me an unexpected bonus had been the wonderful relationship he now had with his dog. I was puzzled, unable to see the connection.

Well, he explained, I know just how my dog feels, I was so frustrated as a baby because I understood perfectly everything that was being said, but could not make myself understood in return. All I could do was scream, a dog must feel just the same as a baby, how he must long for the gift of speech.

This put a whole new light on Human/Dog communication for me. Hitherto I had only thought of *my* frustration in trying to make my dogs understand me. It had never crossed my mind that they too could feel frustrated trying to get what they wanted to say across to dumb old me!

I became much more aware and found that I *could* get messages from my canine friends that had hitherto been lost to me. At the time, my most constant canine companion was Cindy, a Labrador/Red Setter cross. People thought I was being facetious when I told them that she was an irritating back seat driver because of her habit of commenting when I did anything wrong, but my daughter, who was learning to drive at the time, complained bitterly about having a dog sitting in the back seat who criticised her driving!

Cindy, who usually sat bolt upright in the centre, had a way of making an odd, yawny sort of noise (it really did sound as if she was having a go at human speech) if the driver did anything wrong; ground the gears, braked too sharply, went too fast, detoured from the normal route or drove past the pet shop without stopping for dog meat!

I found, after I took more notice of the circumstances when she made this trying to talk noise, that she really was saying something and not just making it at random.

Today I live with another dog who sometimes makes this noise. I try to make out what she is trying to tell me, but sometimes it takes me a long time to get the message, like the time I was so deaf when she was telling me I had forgotten to bring Tara home. Ashley is a Labrador/Cocker Spaniel cross. I wonder if it is coincidence that both my talking dogs should be part Labrador; the breed that is very intelligent, responsible and responsive, one of the reasons why so many of them have successful careers as Guide Dogs for the blind.

The dog is not only Man's best friend, he is also an invaluable assistant and co-worker in so many fields of endeavour. The original common interest that drew Man and Dog together was hunting; not for sport but survival. As time passed and Man became a herder rather than a hunter, the role of the dog changed. His hunting and chasing instinct was channelled into herding and for many thousands of years, wherever Man has farmed livestock, the dog has been there helping him control his herds, whether they were cattle, sheep, reindeer or whatever, the more difficult the terrain, the greater the need for dogs.

Often the dogs work hard for long hours, but sometimes the job can be quite cushy. When I was a child living on a farm in the English Midlands, our cowman had a wise old Border Collie whose one job each day was to fetch the cows up for milking. First thing each morning, Harry would put the kettle on and let Mack out. By the time the dog had the herd ready for him, he had made and drunk his early morning cuppa.

Even though I had been brought up on a farm with working dogs, I was amazed when I first came to Australia, to see Kelpies hop onto the top of a mob of sheep and run with amazing skill and agility along their woolly backs from one end of the mob to the other.

Dogs are still used to aid man in his pursuit of other animals, from the large packs of foxhounds to the single dog out with his master and a gun. Many of our better known breeds were originally bred and developed as hunting dogs of one sort or another. The hounds, which were bred to actually chase and hunt down their quarry, were bred for speed while Labradors and Spaniels were bred primarily to retrieve game shot by sportsmen.

Today, with the changing level of consciousness which has given rise to anti-blood sports societies, many of these so-called sporting breeds, are kept primarily as companion animals and the Labrador is now used extensively by the Guide Dogs For The Blind Association. They have proved exceptionally suitable for this role; physically, they are the right size and their short coat needs little maintenance. Generations of training and close association with mankind in the sporting field has developed a dog with a high level of intelligence and willingness to cooperate. Anyone who has ever watched a blind person confidently negotiating busy city streets with the aid of a dog, must have marvelled at the understanding and communication that must exist between the two.

So successful have these seeing eye dogs become that dogs are now being used extensively in other caring ways. Hearing dogs for the deaf is one of these. Dogs who show a natural aptitude for this work, whatever their breeding or lack of it, are used and trained to tell their owners when the phone or door-bell rings (and which it is), when the whistling kettle boils or the alarm goes off, in fact, any one of the important sounds of daily living.

We have a charming little terrier who came into our family eleven years ago as an abandoned puppy barely five weeks old. For many years she has taken upon herself the task of telling us when the phone rings, she does this by jumping up and running in the direction of the phone, looking over her shoulder and giving shrill yaps to reinforce the message.

As my husband is rather deaf, this is a great help; she has even told him the phone is ringing when he has been busy in the garden. Zoe learned to do this completely on her own. It is easy to imagine how invaluable a dog, carefully chosen for its inborn aptitude for the role, could be to someone with seriously impaired hearing.

Dogs are also now being used to help people confined to wheelchairs by learning to fetch and carry for them, providing not only valuable assistance but wonderful companionship as well. As we become more aware of the capabilities of dogs, so the range of tasks they can do expands. One of the latest discoveries is that some gifted dogs are able to detect when a sufferer from Epilepsy is about to have a seizure and by warning them, they can frequently save them from self-inflicted injury.

We talk about training these remarkable dogs; educating would be a better word to use but it is an education that begins first with the teacher who must develop excellent communication skills in order to get the message across. The fact that dogs now do so many and such varied jobs shows an improvement in people rather than dogs!

We know only too well that if we want to be successful in life, then we should do something for which we have a natural aptitude and liking. Exactly the same applies to dogs, the most successful ones are those who are using their inborn gifts and traits of character.

A large percentage of Guide dogs are bitches, their natural maternal instinct is being channelled into caring for their owner. But whatever the partnership between man and dog, whatever task they do together, the bottom line is always communication. The human must be able to get the message over to the dog and in return the dog must be able to answer back. A partnership between Guide dog and blind person would not be very enduring if the human could get the message across to the dog to cross the road but could not receive a reply in the negative, the information that it was not safe to cross at this particular time. Just as we are giving messages to our dogs all the time, giving the information and commands, so our dogs are talking to us, giving us information.

If we are blessed with good enough memories to travel back in time to our infancy, or very early childhood, we will know that we understood a great deal more than we were able to express. The same goes for a dog. Though his actual vocal speech may be confined to barking, growling or whining (he probably has a pretty good range of sounds in all three), his understanding of our language of words can be much wider. The average dog would have a vocabulary of anything from 30 - 60 words (depending on how much he is spoken to) that he understands. Add to this his observance and reading of other signs, the sound of car keys being picked up, observing whether you are wearing going to town or walking in the bush clothes and all the other little signs, your average dog is pretty cluey about what is going on around him.

It is quite easy to test just how much *your* dog knows; try jingling your car keys, opening the refrigerator or collecting a can opener from the drawer, any one of a number of sounds that could give a message to your dog, then try throwing a few key words into the conversation. Spelling in front of the dog is not a joke, it is something many people have to do if they do not want their dog to slink off at bath-time or have some other inappropriate (to the owner's mind) reaction.

Every dog, from the moment it leaves the security of mother and nest, is looking for one thing; a person to call their own, to love and to look up to as they go through life.

Bob, who was the farm dog on the English farm of my childhood, did not have such a person. He loved, and was loved by, my brother and I, but we were his siblings. Then he met Filipe, an Italian prisoner-of-war from the nearby camp who was assigned to work on our farm.

Children and animals are often credited with being good judges of character. I don't think this is actually so much a question of judgment as such, as a sort of clear seeing. Children, until taught by their elders to do otherwise, do not judge people by the trappings of worldliness that surround them. They see with a clearer vision the real person, the inner self, and can often detect insincerity as if it were a bad smell. Dogs, I think, have much the same ability, perhaps even more so for they are subjected to even less influence.

When I philosophise about War, I remember Filipe and reflect on the criminal absurdity of a situation that made this kind and gentle man, who knew absolutely nothing about world politics, our enemy.

Bob and he seemed to gravitate together right from the beginning. It was Filipe who cradled him in his arms and wept over him when Bob's fascination with moving wheels got him run over. Filipe who beamed with joy and pride when a resilient Bob, after a complete recovery from an accident that would surely have killed a lesser dog, climbed the ladder propped against the rick where he was stacking hay. He boasted with justifiable pride that Bob had learned the somewhat difficult feat of climbing ladders in order to be with him.

Inevitably, the time came when the war ended and the Italian prisoners were repatriated. Tears gleamed in Filipe's eyes as he bade us goodbye. Bob, as usual was standing close at his side. As he looked down at the handsome dog gazing up at him with such love and trust, the tears spilled over and he dropped to his knees and with his arms holding Bob close, he buried his face in the thick golden coat. "Goodbye, my friend! My *best* friend in England!"

Chapter Six

Cat Conversation

Cats and man have enjoyed each other's company for some seventeen thousand years which accounts for the fact that cats are excellent conversationalists. During this long association, they have adopted ways of talking with us that they do not seem to use when dealing with their own kind. Cats do not usually rub against each other as they will against a human leg, or pat one another with a paw to get attention as they will with their special human being.

In some ways, cats use kitten talk in their communication with us. This is natural because we have taken over the role of parent to the cat, and as such, have kept it a perpetual juvenile. The kitten with its mother expects a secure nest, regular feeding, warmth and protection; security. When we take a cat into our home, we undertake to provide those same things. We replace the mother, so, quite naturally, its basic communication with us is much the same as it would have been with her.

The cat cries when it is hungry and purrs when it is satisfied. If it is fortunate enough to have a responsive human substitute parent who is willing to learn, then, as time goes by, the level of communication between the two can develop to conversation standard if the cat is not too taciturn and the human reasonably intelligent and willing to learn.

*4 month old Tara in the first few hours of bonding with me as
her ⌀mother⌀. The wide, anxious eyes betray her feelings at the
loss of her feline mother and the clinging claws her new
attachment to me*

In addition to their voice, cats have three sophisticated and highly developed aids to communication; ears, eyes and whiskers. A cat's eyesight is so good that it can recognise its owner at a distance of 100 metres; its hearing is so good that it can hear a mouse at about 20 metres or at 10 - 15 metres if it is asleep. It can detect sounds that are out of our range, hence the high pitched squeak of a mouse that would be inaudible to the human ear could easily be heard by a cat. Not only can it detect sounds outside our hearing range but in its own voice it has a range beyond our normal hearing span.

Cats have such a wide vocal range, and some, such as Siamese, talk so much that there have been several attempts to actually compile a sort of dictionary of cat language. To the best of my knowledge none of these have been published in dictionary form, if they were I wonder whether they would be displayed for sale among the animal books or alongside the foreign language dictionaries.

Cats are wonderful con artists and past masters of bluff; from blowing themselves up to what appears to be double size and hurling insults and invective at the neighbours cat who has dared to set paw in their territory, to the sweet household moggy who has managed to terrorise their hapless owner into feeding them just what they want.

I know of one cat who supplemented her threatening growling and spitting with biting, her unfortunate person had to wear shoes throughout the summer (however high the mercury climbed) to protect her feet from disciplinary bites! Not so absurd as it may seem, a cat who looks you firmly in the eyes and interjects the odd explosive hiss between the menacing growls can be quite alarming.

Cats have wonderful eyes, in jewel colours and full of expression. Siamese in particular, seem able to flash their sapphire blue eyes in a quite intimidating manner, they also have the advantage of loud voices and a very wide vocal range.

Tara is not really very dangerous at all, just a paper tiger! She has no desire whatsoever to actually engage in paw to paw combat, thanks to her fluent command of feline expletives and her ability to quell an opponent with her piercing Siamese stare, she manages to retain her position as top cat in the family. I have noticed that cats with only part Siamese breeding often manage to hold sway over their companions in a similar way, no matter what they look like, so long as they have inherited the distinctive Siamese voice. These loud authoritative tones obviously fill other felines with deep respect.

If you are a strong enough character and up to living with these emotional prima donnas of the cat world, then a Siamese is an excellent language tutor, for, not only do they talk - loud and long - but actually seem to enjoy holding lengthy conversations with people in general and their own person in particular. Before I had Tara, I had a part-bred Siamese who did not look at all like one, but had inherited the voice and the conversational skills.

At the time I had a small saddle shop located in a little cottage across from the house. Customers wanting the shop would call at the house and if Tabitha was around, she invariably like to trot across to the shop and socialise. She would look into the visitor's face and in a deep throaty voice say Er-woah. I lost count of the number of times recipients of this greeting listened to her in astonishment then asked me in an awed voice; 'Did that cat say Hello?'

Those who knew her simply accepted that was exactly what she was saying, responded to her in like manner and often referred to her as that talking cat.

They were of course absolutely right; that she was consciously imitating human speech I doubt, but she was most certainly saying Hello in cat talk.

There are seven basic sounds in cat language, these are:

1) The miaow or mew, this can range from a casual greeting to an imperious command.

2) The growl, a low menacing rumble not unlike the dogs growl. Used to express anger, anger/fear or fear/aggression. Roughly translated as Back Off!

3) The hiss or spit. More often than not fear with a facade of bravado. It has been suggested by experts in feline behaviour that it could be a direct mimicry of the hiss of a snake, known to strike fear into all. Sometimes there is an underlying note of hysteria in the hiss that seems to say; "Don't push me - I'm at the end of my tether - go too far and I just might explode!" There is a world of wisdom too in the old proverb that reminds us that 't's a cornered cat that spits!'

4) The purr. Commonly believed to mean contentment, so it does up to a point, but it also gives a greater range of more subtle messages than simple satisfaction, like the medieval town crier whose job it was to ensure residents that all was well, the purring cat is expressing her belief that all is well with her particular world (which no doubt explains why we find it such a comforting sound) but a cat can also use the purr in much the same way we use an ingratiating smile; she is giving the message that she is not in an aggressive mood, either because she recognises superior strength or because she knows that she is not up to par. This explains why sick cats may often purr. Definitely the nearest thing in human speech to a purr is a smile, and

Marigold is requesting)or commanding= that a someone)unseen= should open the door for her

just as smiling can mean quite a range of things, so can purring.

5) The caterwaul, this spine chilling and ear-splitting noise used by entire male cats (often in the middle of the night) presages a fight for the favours of a female. It is also used by cats of either sex to warn intruders off their patch and very occasionally aimed at humans who can then consider themselves in *big trouble!*

6) Calling. This is the name given to the distinctive song from somewhere deep in her throat of the lovelorn female.

7) The prrrrt, or chirrup, the soft staccato purr made by the mother cat to her kittens; the male cat to the female he is wooing and occasionally any cat to its owner.

These seven categories of sound are of course only the very basics of cat talk. Each one can be divided and sub-divided again and again.

The miaow for instance can be a soft little mew or a long drawn out yowl of pain, or any one of the many nuances in between. Similarly, the growl can range from a mumbled curse to a battery of expletives delivered at full throttle.

A great deal of cat language has been more or less specially developed for us, the human partner in the person/cat bond. The wide range of miaows is a case in point. Wild cats mew as kittens, just as domestic cats do, but this mewing seldom develops into the large vocabulary of miaows that those who live with a conversational cat can learn (with training) to recognise and understand.

There is the miaow that means "Let me out!" (or in). The one that says "I'm hungry, whats for dinner?" Not to mention the one that complains that what you have just served is not fit for any cat of refinement to eat. There is the miaow of greeting and the one that demands attention. There are also, as astute advertisers of auction sales like to say, sundries too numerous to mention.

Though several attempts have been made to get cat language down on paper, no-one really seems to have been successful but a diligent cat owner, by paying careful attention to their own cats, should be able to gain some fluency in a year or so.

The voice is not the only means cats use to communicate, any more that it is with us humans. Just as we use hand gestures, eye contact, facial expressions, in fact the whole range of body language, to add weight to the messages we are giving verbally, so do cats, and just as individual people develop their own special mannerisms, so do individual cats. Tara has a rather charming way of resting one hind foot lightly on the instep of the person whose leg she is rubbing against, if, that is, she considers that person a very close friend or for some reason is particularly pleased to see them. It seems to be a sort of feline equivalent of the way we might lay our hand on the hand or forearm of a friend we are pleased to see.

She also has a particularly irritating paw gesture, when offered food which she considers sub-standard, she walks away from it shaking her hind feet in disdain, an action that leaves no doubt of her meaning, it is so similar to the way we humans use our hands to repudiate food that is not to our taste.

Conversation is a two way exchange; it is not a question of one participant talking and the other listening. This is something we are all apt to overlook in our communication with our four footed friends.

Take one sound only, the miaow of your cat, and for one day only, listen to it, *really* listen, take note of the various tones and what they mean. If you want to get hooked on the exercise then use a notebook and pen, to make it a really good assignment add a tape recorder. This will make the whole job quite a lot easier because it is far from simple to transfer cat talk to paper.

Be absolutely honest when doing this, if you do not know what your cat is talking about, then record not understood or do not know against that particular comment.

If you have a pretty good relationship with your cat, you will almost certainly know what is being said more often than not. I am also willing to bet that you will note with chagrin that a very large percentage of the messages received and understood are commands. Things like 'Let me out'!, 'Let me in!', 'Breakfast!', 'Dinner!', 'Turn the heater on!', 'Turn the vacuum off!' and probably 'Leave a cat to snooze in peace'. If it is any consolation to learn what you have always suspected, that you are nothing more than a slave to a tyrant in a tabby coat, you can at least congratulate yourself on being an apt pupil.

If cats, over the years, have developed a whole language just to communicate with us, then we too, have learned something about communicating with them. We temper our human arrogance as the supposedly superior species and treat the cat with some deference, even the name Puss is said to be a derivative of Pasht, the title given to the great cat headed goddess of Ancient Egypt. We call her coaxingly, not with the sergeant-major's bellow with which we often summon the dog, and when she strolls in, 2 hours late, we welcome her with joy and relief and offer a slice of chicken.

Those of us who love cats, tend to have a quite slavish devotion to them. We *know* they are selfish and self-centred, but instead of minding, we are pathetically grateful for any small show of affection they may care to bestow upon us. I know Tara sleeps down my bed because it is a lot warmer and more comfortable than her own, yet as she snuggles against me and her deep purr thrums in my ear, I feel a warm sense of togetherness with my little friend. There is, after all, a rather special quality in the company of a cat!

Chapter Seven

Eavesdropping

When we think of the super senses of our dog and cat it is the wonderful eyes and vision of the latter and the remarkable sense of smell of the former that come to mind. We tend to forget that both have far better hearing than we do.

Sound is measured in cycles per second (cps). We humans can hear up to about 20 thousand; as children we have a higher range. My father always used to tell me that he could hear bats until he was 8 years old. It is probable that today's children will lose the ability to hear sounds above 20 thousand cps earlier than their grand-parents because they are subjected to a barrage of sound from an early age. The horse drawn pre-radio and television world of a generation or so ago was not as noisy as today's world.

Cats, it is commonly held, can hear up to 50 thousand cps and dogs 35 - 40 thousand, both considerably higher than ourselves though nowhere near as high as mice who are believed to hear sounds up to 95 thousand cps; no wonder our domestic cats have learned to walk on cushioned paws!

Tara can hear the click of the gas heater being switched on in the lounge when the door is shut and she is a hall-way and another room away. The small click probably sounds like a gun shot to her, and, ever mindful of her creature comforts, the sound invariably brings her to the lounge door demanding admittance.

Cindy, the back seat driver, loved going out in the car almost more than anything. Probably because she enjoyed telling me where to go and how to drive, or not to drive as the case may be. If she was anywhere in the house it was almost impossible to pick up the car keys without her hearing and presenting herself; eager, ready and waiting.

Try opening a can or even picking up a can opener without being heard by your pet. Almost certainly, your dog, and cat, will hear the click of the garden gate before the visitor arrives on the doorstep. They not only hear a car before it turns into the drive gate, but know whether it is a family car or a visitor. Dogs hate sudden loud noises which makes them good guard dogs, they are galvanised into action and retaliate by making a noise back.

We must at times seem unbearably noisy and strident to our little friends, it is a wonder they tolerate us.

Dogs are great listeners; out in the wild eavesdropping is part of their survival kit. A dog must listen for his enemies and he must also listen for his food. A rustle in the grass can betray the presence of either, or both. The dogs who live with us have carried this listening skill over into their present domesticated way of life. It is a skill which we humans are more than willing to utilise.

Thousands of dogs throughout the world are employed as guard dogs to give us early warning of any strangers approaching. Their ability to hear and to listen combined with their chasing or herding instinct makes sheepdogs good at their job. They can hear instructions whistled or shouted from much farther away than we could, with a silent dog whistle they can hear them when even the person blowing the whistle can't! As dogs and cats can both hear sounds beyond our hearing range, it seems only reasonable to suppose that they can also make sounds that are possibly inaudible to our mere human ears. While hearing a wide range is of value for survival, the ability to make them back is important for communication purposes. Cat's ears are set on their heads in such a way that they can hear sounds from most angles without having to turn their head, as we do. Another aide to survival; for an immobile cat waiting for brunch to put in an appearance can hear any sound without the necessity to move at all and thus betray her presence.

I recently witnessed Tara's hearing ability in action at 2 oclock in the morning. It was actually during the writing of this book, I woke in the wee small hours with an idea in my mind, I wanted to get it down on paper knowing from past experience that turning over and going to sleep means total oblivion for that particular thought, I sat up in bed and began to commit it to paper. There was the sudden thump of a cat landing heavily off furniture onto carpet, I looked up from my keyboard and gazed in astonishment at Tara who had a mouse firmly clamped between her jaws. My eyes met hers, and I had no difficulty in reading the message in their glittering blue depths. 'Shall I give it you in bed?'

I have never got out of bed so quickly at 2 am.

"No!" I commanded, "Don't you dare!" I swept her up, mouse and all, and holding her at arms length hurried down the hallway to the bathroom, halfway there she felt it slipping and put up one paw in a most human gesture to prevent if falling.

I have no idea what a mouse was doing in the bedroom but it must have betrayed itself with a fatal squeak, possibly when I switched on the light. I was reminded of the Irish monk who was reputed to have penned the following verse in the Middle Ages:

I and Pangur Bann, my cat,
'tis a like task we are at.
Hunting words I sit all night,
Hunting mice is his delight.

The important facts of life do not change, we scribes and our cat companions are much the same today as then!

There is no doubt that one of the main occupations of todays domestic dogs who are kept as house pets is eavesdropping. They spend a great percentage of their time just listening in to our conversations, as a result they are remarkably well informed about what goes on in the family. Much of this information is gleaned from the tone and pitch of our voice. They know when we are angry or quarrelling, and with whom.

When I was a young adult, still sharing the family home, my parents had a truly wonderful Boxer bitch. Becky really did seem to understand every word we said, we often had to spell in front of her, she also expected a high standard of behaviour, one to another, if two members of the family were quarrelling, or even arguing, she would move between them, curl her lip and even growl at the one who she considered the aggressor. She had no favourites in the family but loved us all alike.

My sister had taught Becky to speak, an achievement I had reason to greatly appreciate one cold and frosty night when I arrived home from a ball around 1.30 am to find my notoriously absent minded father had locked me out! Becky of course got up from her bed in a corner of the big farmhouse kitchen to greet me, I could hear her welcoming snuffles on the other side of the door, but no way could I rouse any other member of the sleeping household, and Becky, clever though she was, could not let me in.

I went outside and yelled outside my parents' window, no response, through chattering teeth I asked Becky to bark; at first the only response was a deafening silence, even the snuffling ceased. I could picture her broad face crumpling in puzzlement. In my thin ball gown with only a light wrap I was frozen, but I managed to get my desperation across to her over the chatter of my teeth. She barked, and kept barking, till my father appeared. I don't know which was greater, my gratitude to her or her delight at seeing me when the door opened.

When my own children were at primary school, another amazing dog entered our lives. Heidi, the German Shepherd, just walked in one day from out of the blue. There were no clues at all to her identity or where she had come from. She was a mass of anomalies; painfully thin with a new scar on the inside of her leg, she was wearing a brand new collar that would probably have gone round her scraggy neck twice, but it had no identifying tag on it at all.

She greeted us like old friends, attaching herself particularly to my eldest son, Graham, who was about 9 years old at the time. Quite calmly she walked into the house with him and sat down by him on the sofa. I told her that was not on, she was too big to sit on sofas, come to that she was too big to be a house dog, and anyway she was not really our dog at all!

We fixed up what we thought was a comfortable kennel in a little yard outside. Her idea of comfort did not coincide with ours. She jumped out of the yard and came back in the house. We tied her up, she slipped her collar and jumped out of the yard and came back in the house. In the end I compromised with her, she could come in the house, but not on the furniture. She agreed, and never got on the furniture again - when I was watching. Occasionally however, I caught her out, usually on my bed, so relaxed was she in her doggy dream world that she forgot to listen for me, when that happened she would look the picture of guilt and try hard to look as if she was invisible, not easy for a taller than average German Shepherd!

Soon she was coming everywhere with us; she achieved this by simply slipping any collar, however tight, and jumping any obstacle, however high, and following the car if we left her outdoors or doing so much damage if left indoors that we just took her along.

Where she came from always remained a mystery, no-one in the little township where we lived had ever seen her before, no German Shepherds were advertised as lost in the papers. It was quite obvious that she had been used to living in a house and from her attachment to Graham we assumed that she had known a boy around his age. She loved riding in the car but was totally paranoid about moving cars that she was not in.

From this we guessed that she had either been dragged into a moving car or thrown out of one. She also had a rooted dislike of a certain type of man. Tallish, thickset, balding, middle-aged to elderly and with a liking for brimmed felt hats. Throughout her long life she never got over this phobia.

We once had some friends from New Zealand staying with us for a week. The husband was the absolute prototype of Heidi's bete noir. For their entire stay she growled every time she looked at him, I found it most embarrassing.

Heidi was an inveterate eavesdropper; I only had to mention in conversation that I was going shopping and she was there, ready and waiting. One hot summer afternoon she was lying in the cool of the hallway some distance from the kitchen, my husband asked me when I was going into Maldon to do the shopping.

In a minute. I replied, and there was Heidi. I had not picked up the car keys, changed my clothes, picked up my shopping basket or even mentioned the word car. The only way she could have known was by listening to our conversation. Cindy, who also loved to travel in the car, was quite blatant in her eavesdropping.

When I had three teenagers in the house, I was, like most parents living in the bush, an unpaid taxi driver. When the phone rang Cindy sat by me - listening waiting for those magic words. I'll come and get you! By the time I had picked up the car keys she was usually waiting at the door.

A rather amusing case of a dog listening in happened a few years back with our brainy little Poodle, Ginger. We had a donkey jenny with a newborn foal in the paddock by the house. Ginger, always curious, wanted to inspect the new baby. Clara, the ever vigilant mother was damn sure she wasnt going to let him. She did not care for dogs at the best of times, when she had a new foal they were anathema to her.

Ginger was told repeatedly to come out of the paddock but convinced as usual that *he* knew best he took no notice. Then there was an angry snort, a thud of hooves and the air was rent by piercing and continuing dog shrieks, yelps and howls as Ginger scrambled through the fence between the paddock and the garden with more speed than dignity. His retreat was not helped by the fact that he was only using three legs.

He stood in front of us, one leg lifted from the ground and hanging in a most ominous fashion, and whimpered. It was the most realistic depiction of a broken leg any of us had seen. "I'll have to take him to the vet!" I cried; And on a Sunday afternoon too!

I had barely said the words before he was off, on his way to the car. Alas - he forgot about the broken leg and ran briskly there on all four paws. There was a gale of laughter from the family; Ginger looked embarrassed and suddenly remembered he had a broken leg, but his sheepish expression and the

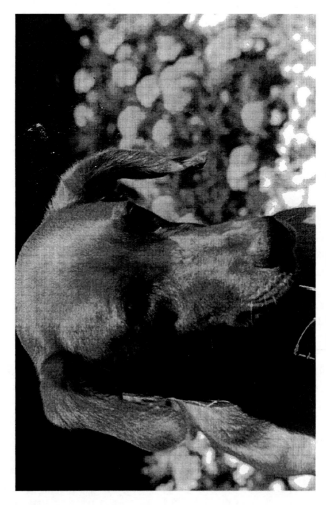

Cindy was a blatant eavesdropper

small ingratiating wiggle of his tail made it clear that he did not really expect to be believed a second time, he knew he had well and truly blown it!

The great stumbling block in accurately assessing just how much our animal friends *do* know is our inability to *really* communicate. We can say that an animal has a vocabulary of 20 words because it responds to that number of words when given verbal commands or otherwise clearly indicates that it knows the meaning of a word. We cannot ever be sure just how much our dog or cat has picked up in years of listening to our conversations. Is it feasible that you or I could spend a great deal of our time listening to people conversing in a foreign language without picking up quite a vocabulary of words?

When we are confronted by unexpected knowingness in our cat or dog, we all too often dismiss it with the airy assumption that they are gifted with some supernatural sense; the reality is that they are using their natural senses to a high degree and that a brain that is brighter than we sometimes realise, is interpreting the information received and coming up with the correct information. It is a salutary thought that our eavesdropping pet may know a great deal more about us than we could ever imagine!

Ginger, who always thought he knew best

Chapter Eight

Calling The Shots

Pet owners often claim that their cat or dog understands every word they say. I know I have said this myself. If we really believe this then it behoves us to be careful what we say. The phrase; 'Little pitchers have big ears' could apply equally to our pets as our children! Fortunately our dogs and cats cannot repeat our remarks at a later date, often to our embarrassment, although I have heard of parrots doing this. The longer I live with cats and dogs the more convinced I become that they *do* understand, if not every word certainly the general drift of what we are saying to them.

Animals however are masters of bluff and are often just as keen to train us to their ways as we are to train them to ours. Therefore it is important that you make it known early on in your relationship just who actually calls the shots. This does not mean taking an arrogant or bullying stance, merely making it quite clear that there are certain house rules that have to be obeyed. You are the one who foots the bill at the veterinarian, the pet shop and pays the licence, you have a right to lay down a few ground rules. It is quite surprising how many people have their lives organised by their cat or dog!

For ten years I ran a small bookshop; Tara always came with me to work. I first took her on the Monday after I had her because I did not want to leave a small kitten alone less than 24 hours after she had joined the household. It was such a success; she enjoyed going and customers enjoyed meeting her that she continued to be a 9 - 5 working cat. She loved the social life, greeting old friends and making new ones and never forgot anyone, giving people she had no't seen for some time such a warm welcome that it was quite obvious that she was pleased to see them. However she had one quite infuriating habit. She thought it most amusing to hide when it was time to go home. I put up with this, playing her game of looking under chairs and round corners for a long time till the evening I had been working very late; in fact it was after 11 pm when I was ready to leave. I picked up my keys and looked round for Tara, exasperatingly when she saw we were going she leapt up onto the top of a very high cupboard, where she knew I could not reach her. She looked down at me with, I swear, a fiendish grin, Certainly her blue eyes were glittering with enjoyment. At this time of night I was *not* amused!

First I asked her nicely to come down, she merely looked back at me with an infuriating "Get me if you can" expression on her face. As she well knew I couldnt get her, but I could leave her! "Come down!" I commanded tersely "Or I shall go home without you!" She stayed and I left. I could hear loud Siamese shrieks and wails as I stepped out of the car the following morning. She was waiting just inside the door as I turned the key in the lock. It did not need much expertise in animal communication to roughly translate her loud and voluble tale of woe. It had been a terrible night, she did not like being all by herself and the top of the cupboard was cold and draughty and uncomfortable, how she had longed for the warmth and safety of the bed she usually shared with me!

This happened several years ago, and if you think it illustrates her lack of understanding you would be wrong, for since that night I only had to threaten to go home without her and she was either at my feet or actually *in* her travelling box!

70

All that time wasted over the years playing Taras game of Hide and Seek when all I had to do to stop it was call her bluff!

We all like to get our own way, whether we are people or pets, however to get it all the time makes us feel not secure, but very insecure. Boundaries are an important part of life. We feel a comforting sense of security when we close the door of our home and are safe within its four walls.

Just as we need physical security so we also need limits and boundaries on our behaviour. It is important to know what we can and cannot do, what is acceptable and what is not.

Children who have parents who give in to their every whim and tolerate intolerable behaviour are seldom happy. In our personal relationships a person who gave into us all along the line would soon become very dull and boring and we would find ourselves looking around for someone else! In just the same way we cannot expect our dog or cat to afford us respect, or even find us very interesting if we give in to them all the time!

To have a successful relationship with our pet we need to know, understand and accept two things. The first is what do we, personally require and expect of our pet? If obedience is high on the list then we should certainly steer clear of all cats and those dogs who tend to be opinionated and independent, such as many small terriers, Pekingese and some small Poodles. However if we think of these characteristics as showing character and initiative then we would get along very well with most members of these breeds. For devotion to duty and obedience then we need to look at the breeds who excel in canine careers that require a high level of training. We find many Labradors working as Guide dogs and German Shepherds doing Police work for example.

To form a successful relationship with our pet we then have to look at things from their perspective and ask 'What are they looking for in a relationship with us?' Understanding these two needs, theirs and ours, and acting accordingly is the basis for a good relationship with our pet, be it cat or dog.

By nature the dog is a pack animal; conditioned to life in a pack with a pack leader. One moreover who expects subservience and who everyone in the pack expects to obey.

When a new puppy joins a family it becomes *his* pack. He must find his place in it and learn the pack rules and obey them. In a human family his place is *not* as leader. However a strong-minded and intelligent pup who finds himself in a family or pack who seem to him to lack leadership qualities will make a bid to be top dog himself. This can be quite disastrous, for a dog who thinks he is in command of everything and everyone in his own little world is not at all nice to know. However given a good leader, who he can look up to and respect, who is fair and kind but above all firm, these natural leaders are wonderful dogs.

Cats, on the other hand, do not live in packs under the dominion of a leader. Although some of the big cats, such as female lions, may join together, the cat is basically solitary and independent. The young kitten that we bring into our home however has lost its nest and its nurturing mother; it is looking for a substitute. So when we take a kitten into our home we take on this role and our home becomes the new nest.

As a mother we are looked to for warmth, food and a set of rules to live by. By providing these, and continuing to provide them, we not only satisfy our kitten's immediate needs but tend to keep it in the role of child to our parent for the rest of its life. Keep your side of the bargain, provide a warm nest, regular meals, lay down a few (very!) simple ground rules and give your affection unstintingly (albeit of a parental kind) and you will be rewarded by a happy and loving pet.

When Tara first came to live with me I made one rule very clear. She never went outdoors after her last meal of the day, whatever the time of the year. This means that I never have to call her in at night and that once in I do not have to worry either about her safety or that of small native nocturnal creatures. Good relationships between pets and people, just the same as people to people relationships, do not just happen; they have to be worked on.

You cannot go out and buy a dog and in so doing purchase for yourself instant love, loyalty and devotion. Nor can you bring a cat into the home and have a cosy, cossety companion overnight. There is every reason to expect that they *will* fulfil these ideals and be everything you dream of in a pet if you are prepared to put a good deal into the relationship in the beginning into what is called by most people, 'training' which usually means that the animal is expected to do all the learning and the person all the teaching. Building a relationship however means that both of you are equally involved in the learning process!

The purpose of Dog Obedience Clubs is not to train dogs but to teach owners to train their own dogs. The way to do this is to understand your dog. Watch and listen, get to know the different tones of its bark, the expression in its eyes, the various ear positions and of course the language of the tail. Be sensitive to its moods, bored dogs, just like bored children, do not learn. Dogs have a great sense of fun and play but do not understand or appreciate teasing. While you are getting to know your dog, he is doing exactly the same with you, and the odds are he is a quicker pupil!

We call them pets, these four legged people we take into our homes, but too often we treat them like a teddy bear or a slave, neither of which can be the least satisfactory to the animals because they are neither. We have all met bored disgruntled unhealthy and unhappy little dogs who have almost lost the use of their legs through being carried everywhere, similarly most of us have met the dog owner who believes, and constantly says; You must show the dog who is boss. Curiously enough, these people never seem to keep a dog for long and they do not usually have cats around at all.

A good relationship with your dog - or cat - is one of loving friendship and mutual respect, a relationship in which each knows the boundaries, when you issue a command or say No! in a certain voice you expect to be obeyed and you know your pet well enough not to push it beyond its own particular limits, in whatever direction.

Dog lovers are often accused of spelling dog back to front, but in actual fact that is how many people expect their dog to see them! We are not gods, and it is very debatable whether even the most devoted dog or caring cat sees its owner in anything like such a flattering light but in one respect we do have a god-like power over our pets, the ultimate power of life and death.

A far cry from Ancient Egypt when the cat was worshipped as a Goddess and at the zenith of her power. The punishment for killing a cat then was the death penalty. Puss has never had things so much her way since; a fact of which she is well aware!

If you know that you were once a god, no matter how long ago - well - it is bound to show somewhat in your demeanour commented Paul Gallico's feline heroine, Thomasina in his enchanting novel called *Thomasina*.

Maybe this long past time in our joint histories is still buried deep down somewhere in the subconscious of both Cat and

Man and now and then bubbles to the surface in our relationship with this once divine creature. When we confess to adoring cats maybe we are remembering a time when we did just that in a most literal sense?

Oddly enough the Egyptians who worshipped cats were one of the very few people to actually train them to do a job of work. Ancient papyrus paintings show cats with men in flat-bottomed boats on the reedy waters of the Nile. The cats which look remarkably like present day Abyssinian cats, were on leashes and were trained to retrieve wildfowl shot by the men with arrows or spears and bring them back to the boat. Considering the cat's natural antipathy to water this must be ranked as some achievement.

Since those halcyon days for Puss she has lived with Man more or less on her own terms, firmly declining education or training in the highest sense. Unlike the dog who, over the centuries has evolved and diversified at Man's instigation to enable him to perform so many varied tasks for us with skill and efficiency.

The list of dog professions is awe-inspiring. In police work he catches criminals and sniffs out drugs and bombs; in the caring professions he is increasingly active; Guide dogs for the blind, Hearing dogs for the deaf, fetching and carrying for the physically disabled. He guards our homes and our places of work, gives companionship and support to countless thousands of lonely people, herds our flocks, joins in our sporting activities - the list is endless, wherever there are people there are dogs.

By selective breeding as well as training Man has created a huge diversity in physical appearance in the dog so that he is not only mentally but physically equipped to do the many and varied tasks we ask of him. Contrast this with the cat who remains much as she was three thousand years ago in appearance and who is never expected to do more than catch a few mice occasionally, which she would do anyway, and be a tolerably pleasant companion. which she does when it suits her. It would seem that the cat made a far better bargain with Man than did the dog.

However the ultimate success of each and every situation in which a human and a dog (or a cat) are thrown together depends entirely on the quality of the relationship between the two of them, and this in turn depends on the level of communication and understanding that develops between them. This is why police dogs live with their handlers, the closer the bond between them the better they work together.

Over centuries of living with Man, the dog and cat have developed somewhat different relationships. The dog, ever eager to please, has become Man's willing partner, co-worker, helper, slave. The cat, on the other hand, has retained much of her independence, even her wild ways. She is an anomaly, a domestic animal who (some would say) is useless. She has not been domesticated to be eaten, for her coat or to work. Valued at one time for her skill in hunting and exterminating vermin, even that is now considered a negative quality. The hunting cat, alas, has not learned to discriminate between vermin and endangered native species, and anyway, Man, the supreme exterminator, has developed enough poisons to wipe out vermin, natives, cats and all!

Yet cats are still with us, useless, untrained, disdainful, they do not even have the grace to be suitably servile. We give them board (the best), bed (often our own), pay their medical bills (no health service for cats). We pour on them boundless affection, and *hope* for a little in return. They do absolutely nothing for our self esteem, dogs on the other hand can bolster the most flagging ego, there can only be one explanation, somehow the cat has managed to convince us of *her* superiority.

Such a creature must be intelligent, strong minded and very persuasive. But of course, companion animals (how much less condescending to call them that) who share our homes and our lives are important, even though to outsiders they may appear useless. They do much more than stave off loneliness, they give love, as well as being something to love. They are someone to talk to and they listen, for many they are a reason for living. Guardian Angels maybe?

We show our appreciation for these creatures we have chosen to live with us in the intimacy of our homes in a very strange way at times. Not the least in our language. To call a person a bitch or a son of a bitch is an insult, similarly when we describe a person as being catty we are not paying them a compliment. In actual fact, very few bitches are bitchy or cats catty in the sense we have given to these words.

If cats have a grouch about another cat (or anyone else) they usually say it straight out - to their face - in no uncertain manner! As for bitches being bitchy, we only need to look at the ranks of the Guide Dogs for the Blind to see that the word bitch can be synonymous with love, devotion and a level of communication between dog and human that is far above the average of that between one human and another. Maybe it is time we revised our use of these words!

Chapter Nine

The Eyes Have It

One of the most common mistakes we make in our dealings with our animal friends is our assumption that what we see and hear so do they. This is by no means always true. We have better binocular vision than dogs but they have better peripheral vision than us. We have both evolved that way to suit our respective lifestyles. The hunting dog must be able to focus on his prey directly in front of him but does not necessarily have to see each hair or feather in detail; he needs to be aware of any dangers or rival hunters around him

We, as humans, need the ability to focus and see details clearly; how else would we be able to repair watches, do fine needlework or even many of the tasks that are part of our routine daily living? Because blind dogs cope so well; due to their remarkable sense of smell; we tend to consider the vision of all dogs poor and even of little importance to them. This is not so. Dogs have good vision and are particularly observant of moving objects; sight hounds such as Salukis and working dogs like Border Collies have particularly good vision.

Most of us have read scientific reports stating categorically that cats and dogs cannot see colour. Those of us who live with animals and see evidence that they *can*, find this confusing. Both dogs and cats do see colour though their range is not as great as ours and they probably see them in more muted tones than we do. Once more this goes back to their natural, or original, lifestyle. In the wild both canines and felines are hunters and a lot of their hunting is done at dusk; at this time of day all colours tend to be muted.

As a compensation for their inability to see colours as clearly as we can both cats and dogs can see better in dim light. Cats, being truly nocturnal animals, have excellent night vision though they cannot, as is generally supposed, see in total darkness, they have the ability to make the best use of any light available.

The eyes of both cats and dogs are extremely beautiful, but in different ways. The expression:

The eyes are the windows of the soul might well have been written about the eyes of a dog. From them shines intelligence, love and devotion, and strikes a responsive chord in the human looking into them; filling them with a feeling of love and warmth, even inspiring them to put their feelings into verse as I did when I looked into Ashleys beautiful eyes and wrote the following verses:

Unconditional Love

Unconditional Love! Cry the prophets of The New Age.
Unconditional Love; this is the in phrase.
Easy to say; not so easy to give,
This pure and selfless love without strings.
Pondering so, I feel a touch and glance down into twin pools of liquid, speaking brown;
The eyes of my spiritual mentor, my canine Guru;
Saying, not Love me! but Please, may I love you?

I am far from being alone in being inspired to put pen to paper by the eyes of a dog. Poets and writers have been doing it for centuries. We are equally struck by the beauty of cat's eyes, though it is our aesthetic sense here more than our emotions that is touched.

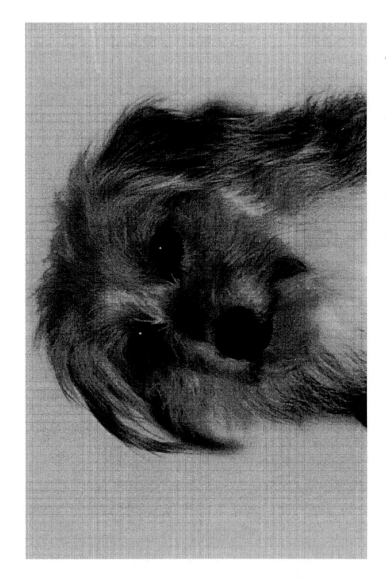

The eyes are the windows of the soul. This applies to dogs as much as people

The beauty of cat's eyes lies both in their shape and their colour. Large and round, often glowing with a wonderful luminous quality, they come in the most incredible range of jewel colours unmatched by any other living creature, including humans. They range from palest honey coloured gold to deepest brilliant amber; from aquamarine and lime green to vivid emerald and from light baby blue through turquoise to deepest sapphire. Whatever colour these wonderful eyes are it is always one that is a perfect compliment to the fur coat worn by that particular cat.

These beautiful eyes are also remarkably efficient. They can make the best possible use of any light that is available; detect the slightest movement in their surroundings and can recognise their own particular person at a distance of 100 metres, they can also observe and take in detail as the following shows.

In the early days of Tara's life as a shop cat I had a red Ford Laser. It so happened that the couple who ran the sewing shop next door to my bookshop had an almost identical car. A friend of mine was holding Tara in her arms looking out through my shop window as she chatted to me. Suddenly Tara's attitude changed dramatically. The contented purring stopped and became a menacing growl; Her body stiffened, out came her claws and into friends shoulder, her tail took on a furious life of its own; her neck seemed to grow twice as long, and her ears twice as big and her eyes, out on stalks, became glittering points of fury fixed on something outside the window.

The change was so sudden and so dramatic that our conversation was halted in mid sentence and I hurried to the window to see what on earth had caused her to be so enraged. Just outside the window the man from the next door shop was getting into *his* red laser, which Tara had obviously mistaken for *her* red laser and which she imagined was being stolen! As she was always carried into and out of my car in her enclosed travelling case I would not have expect her to be so cognisant of the cars outer appearance (nor so possessive) apart from the number plate, which of course she could not read, the two cars were just about identical.

Heidi, the German Shepherd who did not like bald men in felt hats, failed to recognise my daughter on two different occasions. Each time she had been to the hairdresser and had a complete change of style. Proving, not her inability to recognise, briefly, someone she knew very well, but that dogs, like us, must rely a good deal on what they see when they look at a person on a day to day basis.

You will realise how true this is if you take the trouble to notice your dog's reaction to the different clothes you wear. You will soon see that he or she is very well aware which clothes mean you are going to work and which shoes, or coat, or whatever, you put on for dog walking. Long before you actually pick up the leash he will be pretty sure that an outing for him is in the offing.

Watching the expression in your dog's eyes can be a very enlightening and rewarding pastime. But be careful never to stare directly into his eyes. In the animal world this means aggression and the last thing you want to do is appear to threaten.

Dogs on the whole are straightforward and honest, though it has to be admitted that they can be capable of surprising guile at times. However generally speaking what you see in the eyes reflects what is going on inside the mind and heart of your dog.

You will find it an interesting exercise to take your note-pad and biro and jot down all the many facial expressions, or looks, your dog has and against them record what you imagine he is saying.

An easy example is the bright quizzical look, often accompanied by pricked ears, which quite clearly asks; Well, are we going out? You will soon be able to distinguish between that and the similar look that means, Dinner? and will quickly learn to recognise the sharp responsible gleam that tells you he is in guard dog mode when the doorbell rings.

All of us know only too well that look of sheer tragedy that can induce such feelings of guilt within us when we have to say, "No you can't come today!" and walk firmly away.

When you watch yourself observing your dog you will realise that the communication with you is actually at a much deeper level than the mere giving and taking of orders; and you can be sure of one thing; you, the watcher. are also being watched! Cats may not have the speaking eyes of dogs but their faces are by no means expressionless, inscrutable sometimes, but not without expression, much of which is centred in the eyes, and what she is doing with them.

Half-closed in an almond shape tells you that she is relaxed and at peace with the world. Round as coins she is scared, narrowed and firmly focused she is giving something (you or a mouse hole) her full attention. Open and staring, though not wide with alarm, she is alert and giving her full attention to something out there. An unwavering and unblinking stare probably means she is being aggressive and asserting her authority over the next door cat - or you. Looking directly at you however and slowly closing her eyes in a blink is the cat equivalent of throwing you a kiss.

The glass studs that light up in the glow of traffic lights are called cat's eyes, for obvious reasons. All cats have eyes that glow when caught by light; most yellow/green or orange but the eyes of Siamese and other blue-eyed breeds glow red. Very occasionally the eyes of an orange-eyed cat will also glow like coals.

Tara sitting outside looking in and using the eye powerøto
compell me to open the door

White cats can be either blue or orange-eyed and quite often they can be odd-eyed. Something which looks even more bizarre in artificial light when one eye glows green and the other burns red! I once had such a cat and I used to say that at night her eyes looked like traffic lights!

A friend of mine once had two Siamese cats, a handsome pair of litter brothers who were firm friends. One of the places they loved to sit together was half-way up the staircase, just where the light from the hall caught their eyes. My friend had a Spanish cleaning lady at the time who invariably crossed herself and muttered darkly about devil cats when she looked up and saw four glowing red eyes fixed on her. She did not stay with my friend too long but took another job nearer home (that was her excuse for leaving) de-moralised by the ruby-eyed scrutiny of the devil cats!

As well as having eyes that glow in this unnerving way in artificial light Siamese cats seem to have a remarkable ability to flash their eyes in a very disconcerting way.

I have seen Tara's eyes positively glitter when she is being aggressive in a way I have never seen green or gold eyes. This ability together with the distinctive loud Siamese voice has given Tara the edge in many a feline argument and enabled her to retain her position as top cat in the household without ever having to resort to paw power.

Both cats and dogs use the unwavering stare as a means of gaining the ascendancy over other cats and dogs, and, in the case of herding dogs, over their charges. A good sheepdog is said to have eye, this means that he will fix this unwavering stare on a sheep and not look away until he has induced it go where he wants.

This quality of eye often shows itself at a very early age. On the English farm of my childhood we had a wonderful Border

Collie bitch called Rose. It was always a matter of great pride when one of her pups was seen to bail up something or someone with its eyes in this way. I remember one such pup, still in the roly poly stage and a long way off starting his serious working life, bailing up the large (and quite ferocious) rooster who roamed the farmyard. The small, fat pup, half the size of the bird, had him where he wanted him merely with the power of his eyes.

We have only to watch dogs and cats using their eyes in this way to realise that in dog and cat language staring directly into the eyes of another is a form of aggression and domination and therefore something we should avoid doing when we are out to make friends with a cat or dog.

We can however make use of this knowledge when we do need to assert our authority, such as when it is necessary to impress the importance of a command, maybe even for its own safety, on our dog. For example if our dog were about to run across the street to us we would shout the command 'Stay!', 'no!', or whatever else was appropriate and at the same time give the hand signal it recognised to remain where it was and to reinforce this we would look firmly and directly into its face.

Dogs are just as much aware of the power of the eyes as we are and intelligent, strong-minded ones will deliberately try to avoid direct eye contact with us when they do not wish to obey a command. If Ashley turns her face away and refuses to meet my eyes when I am telling her something important I put a hand on either side of her face and *make* her look at me.

The ability of cats to see a moving object, however slight the movement is phenomenal yet it can be very difficult to draw their attention to something that is stationary. Cats can be quite exasperating in their apparent inability to see a morsel of food placed before them; unlike dogs they do not seem to grasp the concept of a pointing finger, a literal blind spot in a creature which otherwise displays so much intelligence. While a dog will follow the direction of our point we will have to make the object move to get the message across to the cat.

There is a breed of dog called The Pointer. These dogs tell the hunter where the game is by pointing in the right direction with their nose. All dogs point to a lesser or greater extent, The expression *"Just follow your nose!"* was probably coined by a dog!

One of the most remarkable human/animal partnerships in history (the more so because of the many times it is repeated) must be that of the blind person and their Seeing Eye dog. The dog literally becomes the eyes for the person who in return has to invest a great deal of confidence and trust in the animal.

My bookshop had a butcher's shop next door, a bus stop outside the door and a supermarket across the road. I often used to see a blind man with his beautiful chocolate Labrador get off the bus, go into the butchers shop then cross the road to the supermarket before catching another bus.

On two occasions however the dog brought the man into my bookshop instead of the butcher. I can fully appreciate why a dog would take his person into a butcher *instead* of a bookshop, but not the other way round!

The first time it happened the man asked me where he was, told the dog he had made a mistake and off they went to the butcher.

The second time it happened he asked; "Has he brought me into the bookshop *again?*" I assured him that he had indeed. The dog meanwhile was standing there looking foolish, the expression on his face that of one who knows he has made a mistake. As they went out the man was saying to him; "Now - come on; What *do* you think you are doing? You know I said the butchers shop!"

I think the dog had misheard but in doing so he showed his power to see and observe. Sheila Hocken in her remarkable book about her experiences with her Guide dog, *Emma and I* relates how, when she moved to a new district, with only Emma to show her around she simply said to the dog, 'Find a chemist' or a Phone Box or whatever it was she wanted and Emma took her without fail to the nearest one.

I was once told a delightful story about a cat whose owner, an elderly lady, lost her sight. The cat was a beautiful Persian. The lady was a very keen gardener and even after she became blind she still delighted in working among her plants. The cat always stayed close to her; guiding her by just touching her with a plumed tail.

Dogs and cats both spend a lot of time watching but I doubt if we always realise just how often we are the object of this observation.

Our dog usually makes it clear that not only has he been watching out for intruders but also for our return while we have been gone but how often do we realise that a cat is watching?

Spend a bit of time in observation yourself and notice just how often your cat happens to be around when you get home. It is not in the cat's nature to make an emotional fuss when you return but nevertheless she has probably spent hours sitting under a bush with the drive gate in her sight or sitting in a window sill or on a convenient wall; anywhere that gives her a good view of your return. When I was living in Oxford, England, I shared a first-floor flat with Tiny, a very special little cat.

I did notice that she was always there to greet me when I turned the key in the door and let myself in but assumed that she heard my step on the landing or even coming up the stairs. It was only when my landlady told me that she always knew at least 5 minutes before I got home that I was on the way that I realised her vigil was longer than that. It took me at least 5 minutes to walk from the end of the road where I either got off the bus or, if I was on foot, turned the corner, and that was when I was visible from the window of my sitting room.

My landlady, whose flat was directly below mine, told me that when she heard Tiny jump down from the windowsill to the floor she knew that I had turned the corner and would be home in 5 minutes. This told me that not only did my little cat watch for me to return when I was out but that she had excellent vision and good powers of observation and recognition. It was a busy residential street with lots of people coming and going all the time, moreover if I came home by bus I was seldom the only one to get off at that point but would be one of a group.

My landlady was an elderly person who spent a good deal of time at home and while I was being watched for by Tiny she herself was being observed. I was working as a free-lance journalist at the time so my comings and going were anything but regular. I was touched to think of the many hours my little friend must spend in her self-imposed vigil. I was also grateful to an observant human being who had brought her behaviour to my attention.

All too often we take both our cat and dog friends and their feelings for us for granted. Maybe if we could spare them a little more attention and particularly take note of the many and varied messages being transmitted by their beautiful and so expressive eyes we could enhance our understanding of, and enrich our relationship with, our small friends.

Chapter Ten

Let's Talk

We have come a long way since Descartes, the 17th century philosopher who shaped so much of Western thinking, made the comment that animals were automatons, incapable of thought or feeling who merely existed for the use of people. Such a line of thought, coupled with that of the Church, who declared them soul-less, gave humans license to treat animals as callously as they wished without disturbing their consciences.

As we become more aware of the other creatures who share Planet Earth with us, we also recognise our interconnectedness and that beneath, or beyond, our differences there is a common thread, we all want to survive and enjoy our living.

The closer your relationship with the cat or dog who shares your home and the better you get to know them, the more you will realise that not only are they very human but we are very animal and it is from this base line of sameness that communication begins.

Talking to your dog usually starts with the commands you give it and expect it to learn and obey. With cats it might well be the other way round, the cat teaches the human a few basic commands and expects it to obey!

There is a considerable difference of opinion about how much cats and dogs actually understand of our language. It is a question we can never answer for sure, without being a dog or a cat ourselves! I think they learn a basic vocabulary, the size of this will vary and be influenced by several factors; the intelligence of the individual animal, the clarity and consistency with which the words are used, the amount of opportunity it has to hear spoken words and connect them with objects or actions and by the matching of words and tone of voice. This last is very important when talking to animals, if you tell Fido in a syrupy voice that he is a naughty boy he is going to get a very muddled message!

If you want your pet to eventually have a large vocabulary, start with a very small one and build up, word by word, just as you would build a wall brick by brick. The very first word your cat or dog should get to know when it comes into your home is its name. Short names with clear vowel sounds are the easiest to learn, if possible try to make it special and not sounding like another pets name. The next word a dog should learn is 'Come', from this base you can gradually build up a vocabulary of basic words such as 'No', 'Good', 'Sit', 'Stay', etc., but while you are busy teaching your dog these building blocks in communication you must also find time to take note of his own particular way of telling you things.

Dogs and cats who live in the house with us as family members hear a veritable barrage of words each day as spoken language ebbs and flows round them, inevitably an intelligent animal is going to pick up quite a few words and know exactly what they mean in relation to themselves.

You can find out some of these by deliberately inserting words which you think your pet knows into the conversation and watch for a reaction, it has been my experience that they reveal their knowledge and understanding more clearly in unrehearsed situations. Maybe they convince us more forcibly at such moments because we are not actually expecting anything.

On one occasion I had chicken scraps for Taras lunch (just about her favourite food) but she was being temperamental and declining to come. Telling her it was chicken caused an immediate about turn, as she trotted into the kitchen it was quite easy to translate her miaows into "Chicken! Well that's different! Of course I am ready for lunch!"

I don't think I have ever had a dog who did not know the two words walk and bath and display joy at the prospect of the former and abject horror at the latter.

Ashley, as well as Tara, used to accompany me to business each day but while Tara came inside and socialised with the customers, and now and then caught a mouse to justify her presence on the payroll, Ashley spent most of her time in the back porch or large backyard guarding the rear entrance. When I arrived first and knew Ruth, my daughter who ran the business with me, would arrive in a few minutes, I left Ashley in my car and the yard gate open so that Ruth could drive straight in. She would let Ashley out of the car when she had shut the gate. I have taught Ashley that she must not hurtle out of a car until told she can get out because to do so can be very dangerous when there is traffic around.

One day Ruth complained that Ashley always flung herself out of the car the minute she opened the door. Almost knocking me over! she said, adding; "What do you say to her when you leave her?" I thought for a moment, carefully recalling the exact words I use. "Stay - till Ruth comes". I was pretty sure that was what I said. Try telling her she is to stay till I *tell* her she can get out. Ruth suggested.

So I changed my instructions slightly and Ruth reported that Ashleys behaviour also changed, she waited until told to get out of the car before doing so, thus proving that not only did she understand the exact wording of the brief instruction I always gave her, but was also capable of following instructions to the letter. This does not mean that she is a very obedient dog, on the contrary, she is highly intelligent and strong minded, two qualities which do not always add up to obedience!

All too often in our dealings with our animal friends, we prefer to ignore the fact that each one is an individual with its own likes and dislikes and an ability to say *no* as well as *yes*.

Anyone is capable of having a one to one conversation with their cat or dog. In fact those of us who live with pets are doing it all the time. It is not a rare psychic ability. All it requires is love, patience and understanding, plus adherence to a few simple rules.

First, when talking to your pet, *keep it simple*. Short words, preferably of one syllable only, repeated often and always used consistently. This rule applies to the animals name too. Do not call it Fido or Fluffy one day and Baby, Honey, Precious or something else the next day. Be careful not to use the same word in a totally different context. For example, if you use the word 'drop' to get your dog to change from a sitting position to a lying one, use a completely different word such as 'give' when you want it to let some object go out of its mouth.

The second cardinal rule is to *listen* (and watch). You expect your pet to do this to learn your vocabulary, only by returning the compliment can you learn his.

True, day to day communication with your pet is not a psychic ability, however there are people who have developed this to an extraordinarily high level enabling them to tune in and, it would seem, pick up an animal's inner thoughts, just as there are people who can do this with other humans. In this

Matilda, who once told me to shut up, tells me to Push off when I crept up on her with a camera to snap her spying on the neighbours back garden

instance it can be classed as a paranormal (above and beyond the normal) or psychic ability.

Can anyone learn to do this? Yes, with certain qualifications, most important your own attitude, particularly towards animals.

This is not a power thing; if you try to get inside an animal's mind in order simply to control it then you are quite likely to find entry barred and shut. Approach with love and a real desire to understand together with a willingness to talk on your pets level and you may get through.

Most young children, *before* they go to school and learn to read, think pictorially, so do animals. There is often a strong bond between small children and animals and the former will often know exactly what an animal is saying. This is not surprising for your dog and child may well be very similar in mental age, whatever their actual ages.

Pre-school children and animals also are operating for a great deal of the time in the Alpha brainwave state, that relaxed, dreamy, non-aggressive (or competitive) frame of mind when we are open to input (often on a subconscious level) from our senses. In this state of mind our intuitive awareness is very much alive and kicking as opposed to our more sensible cerebral sense. In other words, we are in just the right condition to interact with another mind in similar mode.

We all slip in and out of Alpha several times a day; when we first wake up in the morning and lie there in a pleasantly dreamy state, when we relax under the shower, when we just sit - day-dreaming. These are the times when our intuition rather than our logical brain is at work so these are also the times when we get most of our brightest ideas and when we are most in tune with other minds.

Body language! It is easy to see that Cindy has quite deliberately switched off

When you are idly day-dreaming and the idea suddenly comes to you to take your dog for a walk, it is probably not accidental at all, your innocent looking pooch has been sitting there thinking how nice a walk would be and accidentally (or maybe deliberately) put the idea into your head.

You can use this mind-to-mind business the other way too; when you are trying to get some message across to your pet, perhaps you are teaching your dog something, or showing your cat how to use the cat flap you have just installed in the back door, then do your best to get a clear picture in your mind of just what it is you want them to do, hold it there, that is all you have to do, there is no need to try and force project it into their mind, if you can hold a clear enough picture in your own mind, the chances are your pet will pick it up, unless it has deliberately pulled the shutters down!

To pick up messages from your pet in a similar way then you need to relax completely. Try and choose a quiet moment when you and your dog or cat are alone in pleasant circumstances. Sitting by the fire in the evening for instance. Try not to think of anything in particular but let your mind go as blank as possible. Yes, I know that is about the most difficult thing in the world to do.

Our minds are always busy busy with one thought after another chasing through. Use the white screen approach. You can do this either way, you may find it easier to put a picture of what you want to send to your pet on a white screen; but to receive all you need in your mind is your screen, unroll it in front of your minds eye and keep it quite blank. Relax, try and tune into you pet, and watch your screen, you may be lucky and get a picture of what they are thinking. You may even hear words inside your head, as I did when Matilda told me to 'Shut up!'.

Cindy uses a very human gesture to attract my attention

You may of course get nothing, but if this happens don't give up, it may not mean that *you* are totally unreceptive but that your pet is simply not transmitting. There is also the possibility that *they* have a blank screen waiting to receive *you*!

Over the years, there have been many attempts to get animals to talk and almost invariably this means talk in our language, therefore most efforts have been notable failures. Much more successful have been experiments teaching chimps Sign Language. They have proven apt pupils and surprised their teachers with their comprehension of things that it was always thought animals could not understand! We often do our animal friends a disservice in the way we perceive them. We tend to either believe that because they are animals and we are humans there is a vast unbridgeable gap between us and we do not give them credit for the intelligence and built-in wisdom that is part of their make-up.

At the other end of the scale we humanise them and expect them to understand and behave just as we do. The reality is that we are all animals, just different species, with different qualities and ways of communicating. It is as pointless to choose a dog as a companion and not accept it as a dog as it is to choose a Siamese cat because Siamese are dog like. We all, dogs, cats and people, just want to be accepted, and loved, for what we are when it comes down to the bottom line.

Real communication is love in action. It is acceptance, understanding, togetherness, all rolled into one. We have all experienced the feeling of rejection when we are not listened to. Being misunderstood and not listened to is a lonely existence, especially for an only pet who has to rely on humans for companionship.

Words are only one way of talking. We also express a great deal with body language and what I call thought talk. In esoteric circles this is sometimes referred to as direct mind to mind communication; that is a thought, an idea or a message directly transferred from one mind to another without the use of speech or any other form of communication. Most of the time, we are using a blend of all three methods, each underlining the other. Animals do the same and, like us, sometimes rely more on one method than another.By observing our pet's body language and being consistent in the way we use our own we can understand and be understood a great deal more than if we just use speech. This is something every animal trainer, or teacher, knows instinctively.

We have all wished, often aloud, that our pets could talk. They can, and they do, the problem is it is in *their* way, by listening and watching them, instead of concentrating on teaching our dog and cat *our* way, we will have a good chance of finding out what our talking pet is saying, and may even be able to answer back!

Chapter Eleven

A Member of the Family

Students of human behaviour are fond of saying that those who keep cats and dogs have them as substitute children. While this may sometimes be so it is far too sweeping a statement and like many such statements contains an element of truth but by no means the whole truth. Those for whom it is true would be better off with a Teddy Bear or a Raggedy Anne doll, and so probably would the hapless dog or cat!

In the vast majority of families the cats and dogs tend to be rather more just one of the children rather than substitute children; in other words they are part of the family. The nuclear family beloved of children's story-books, has for time honoured generations consisted of Mother, Father, two children, one a boy and the other a girl, and the family cat and dog.

It is not necessarily a bad thing when animals do substitute for children, providing we never lose sight of their dogginess and catness. Like everything else in life, balance, and keeping things in proportion is all important.

One of the great attractions of cats and dogs is their Peter Pan quality. Dogs are a bit like children who remain in that delightful pre-school, or very early Primary school, stage in life. Most experts in canine intelligence and behaviour will say that the average dog has about the same I.Q. as a 4 - 5 year old child. This is a delightful age in children, they have developed a measure of independence, but not too much, and they are good company and fun to be with. No wonder we like having dogs around.

The attraction for us of cats is that we do not *allow* them to grow up. On the contrary we keep them pickled kittens by their dependence on us for food and shelter, in other words we keep them like kittens in the security of the home nest whatever their actual age.

We like cats small, human baby size bodies, their roundish heads and large round eyes, again subtly appealing to the parental and protective in our make-up. Their, for the most part, totally deceptive air of helplessness makes us feel good. Sometimes we even know it is deceptive but we just love them the more for it.

Over the last few decades the popularity of cats as pets has increased to the point where, numerically, they outstrip dogs, particularly in urban areas. Oddly enough it is the flip side of her character, her independence that accounts for this.

The cat, almost more than any other living creature, is the perfect embodiment of the ancient Chinese principle of Yin-Yang. Basically this can be said to be the harmonious blending of opposites into a perfectly balanced whole. When we choose a cat for a pet, that is what we get. We have the helpless baby which appeals to our nurturing side and to offset that we have the self-sufficiency and independence that allows the cat to fit into a busy lifestyle in an undemanding way, as an equal. No wonder today's cat is so often found sharing, and enjoying, the comfortable lifestyle of upwardly mobile business and career people!

The independent side of the cat means that she can be left to her own devices during the day, the dependant part of her will ensure that she is there when her human family returns, ready, like them, to enjoy all the comforts and security of home.

As we approach the end of the twentieth century the average nuclear family beloved of the story books, Mum, Dad, Johnny and Jane, Rover and Tiddles is much more likely to be one single, working parent, which may, or may not, be Mum, and one or two children. Tiddles may well be still there because of her ability to fit in without too many demands. Rover is the one most likely to be dropped because of the greater demands he makes on time and attention, both of which may well be in short supply. If he is still there he is probably larger because in today's world the dog as protector of home and family is increasingly in demand.

It is not only men who seek the companionship of the more macho members of the dog world, many women on their own or with young children, sleep easier at night knowing that a large and protective dog regards the home as very much his territory.

Whatever the make-up of the individual family (I use the word family here to describe any number of people from one upwards, whatever their relationship to each other, who share a dwelling) once the decision has been made to take a cat or dog, whether infant or adult of the species into the household, then it, too, becomes a member of that family.

As such it must have its basic needs met for shelter, food and affection and, like all the other members of this particular family it must get to know, and abide by, the ground rules. These of course vary from family to family but one in particular should be sacrosanct in any group of people (and animals) living together. Each and every one must have its own special place, its own sanctuary, where it can retreat and be undisturbed.

Fluffy, normally a very cossety cat displaying her Yang side, the independent hunter

For most cats and dogs their own special bed that is theirs alone usually provides this haven.

Dogs get very attached to their own bed, in fact this is probably one of the first words a new puppy in the household should learn. Not only is it a sanctum for the dog but it is very useful to be able to send it there when you require it to sit quietly out of the way!

You do not have to spend a fortune on pet furniture, although a look round any good Pet shop will show you that it is very easy to do this if you wish. An old chair in the back porch, a blanket in a special corner or a cardboard box will often fit the bill. Most dogs love beanbags and a vinyl covered beanbag can make quite a good hygienic bed as it is easy to keep clean. Far easier in this respect than the whicker basket so often sold for dogs and cats. A whicker basket is *not* a good idea for a young puppy who is almost sure to chew the sides. I have seen baskets that have ended up more like mats than baskets and those chewed jagged bits of cane sticking out are diabolically hard on clothes and skin!

Cats almost always prefer something they can sit in rather than on. Something which the makers of beds for cats are now realising. For many years Taras bed was a cardboard box that had originally housed a Giant Easter egg. It had three sides, a top and a bottom and a large oval opening at the front. It was a perfect one-cat bed. It was given Tara by a young friend who won the egg in a raffle. She told her mother that she would give the box to Tara because 'she would like it'. How right she was. Tara loved it, from the moment she first saw it, and slept in it for several years till it literally collapsed round her!

Cats not only like beds they can get into but often those where they can get under things as well. A good example of this is the cat that likes to share its owner's bed, particularly on cold nights.

Fluffy sits up, the better to absorb the information left on this bush by a passer-by

When I was sharing a London flat with two cats, one of them, Candy, just loved to crawl up under the cover of the divan which was a couch by day and a bed by night. Even though she was quite a large cat she could wriggle up the side of the cover and into a slight hollow so skilfully that there was no ruffle or wrinkle to show where she had crawled in and no discernible hump to betray her presence once there.

It became an automatic warning to visitors; "Don't sit on the cat!". Those who did not know Candy gave me a very odd look when a quick glance over the chairs to see where they must not sit drew a blank. She was a rather anti-social cat who tended to disappear with the arrival of visitors so more often than not she would be in her rather vulnerable position under the cover of the divan. The sound of a voice at the door or a strange footfall was guaranteed to send her there post-haste.

There were few exceptions, but one of them was my husband (only he was not my husband in those days) I used to tell him that the real reason I decided to marry him was because Candy actually put in an appearance to greet him when she heard his voice. There is many a true word spoken in jest, so the saying goes. As I have always had a healthy respect for the opinions of my animal friends about the humans we both know maybe I was influenced by Candy, just a little!

After all a decision as important as getting married meant a change of home, not only for myself but for the other two members of my immediate family at the time; the two cats who shared my flat and my life. For my opting for marriage meant a change of home and lifestyle for them too.

What would I have done if Candy had displayed real fear and dislike for him? Or, alternatively, if he had refused to accept my two cats along with me? I hope I would have had the good sense to have heeded the warning.

Subsequent events so often prove to us that our little animal friends can be much better judges of character at times than we are ourselves.

I was once telephoned by a complete stranger asking me to help her find homes for her two Persian cats as her soon-to-be new husband refused to accept them. I had actually taken this call in my father's office.

"You should have told her to get rid of the man and keep the cats!" He told me; "She'll live to regret it if she doesnt!". I hope for her sake he was wrong, but I cannot help feeling that it is a poor sort of love that asks a person to give up their little animal friends like that. The cats, I am sure, would have accepted him.

The traditional storybook view of the dog and the cat as both obligatory members of the family circle does has something in its favour. Each bring quite different qualities and both can teach invaluable lessons to the younger members of the family, in particular.

By their very dependence on us they give children a sense of responsibility and foster their own ability to nurture. With animals as part of the family circle the only child can learn to share and care just as well as those who have siblings. Children who live in close proximity to animals can also learn a good deal about love.

Psychologists tell us that we are around 18 months old when we learn the harsh lesson that being loved is, to a certain extent, dependant on being good, or rather in pleasing. But the child sharing a home with a caring and cared for pet will also discover that *their* love can always be depended upon, whether or not Mummy and Daddy are pleased.

Dogs are usually seen much more in this role of emotional comforter; nevertheless the cool cat can also give great support. Marigold, a lovely Tortoiseshell and White cat, formed a strong bond with the small boy she lived with when they were both babies. Most cats make themselves scarce when they hear a small child expressing his anger, frustration or just plain hurt, at full throttle. Not so Marigold, she would rush straight to her small friend, pressing her body as close to his as possible and stay till the tears were stemmed. In fact she was quite often the only one who could achieve this.

Left to themselves without too much adult interference and interpretation young children and animals often understand one another remarkably well.

When my grandson was 3 years old he was staying with me for a few days while his parents were away. He and Ashley love each other dearly. One day, in the way of small boys, he kept persistently pulling her tail. Possibly because it was a convenient height, and a convenient length and was always wagging. He stood directly behind her, grabbed it with both fists, leaned back and pulled. I felt this really was stretching her tolerance a bit and repeatedly told him not to do it, Without apparently getting the message over.

Towards the end of the day, my back was towards them both when a mighty roar from Ashley caused me to swing round, wet dish-mop in hand. The volume of the sound led me to expect Zacs heels disappearing down Ashley's maw, like 'Our Albert' who, you will remember, was eaten by a lion at the zoo in retaliation for being poked with a stick.

What I actually saw was child and dog standing very close, side by side, with identical expressions of sheepish guilt on their faces. Ashley's whole demeanour was one of apology, from the set of her head, the angle of her ears, the look in her eyes and of course the slow waving of her tail. The verbal explanation came from Zac; ""Ashley said Don't pull my tail! he told me", adding, "So I won't". In a few seconds, without doing him the slightest bit of harm, she had finally got over the message I had been doing my best to deliver throughout the day! Furthermore he has never, ever, pulled her tail since, but they remain on the very best of terms.

It would have been so very easy in this instance to have been angry with the dog for making such a horrendous noise which certainly *sounded* most alarming. I was so glad I was not. Ashley, I realise had acted in exactly the same way she would have done had it been a child of her own species annoying her so persistently.

Small children quite often tell us in their own words exactly what an animal is saying. If we observe and listen we may find that their interpretation of dog or cat language is much more accurate than our own!

The close bond between children and pets in the same family is quite often more that of a sibling relationship than the people/pet one.

Looking back down the years to my own childhood I know that I saw Mickey, the family dog as my brother and friend, not really in the light of pet at all, or even really as an animal. Of course I *knew* he was a dog and as such different to me, physically, but I did not see him as inferior in any way, less intelligent or even of less value in the family group as myself. We were different, but equal down to basics, this means knowing and loving the *real* person inside the body. In our close relationship with other humans it is this essence, or inner person, that we have the relationship with, not the external person.

Even though the initial attraction to a person may be physical (just as we may pick the prettiest kitten in the litter) when we really get to know them we move beyond this. We do not keep looking at our nearest and dearest exclaiming; "Gee, you have such wonderful hair, or eyes, or legs, which is the reason I stay with you!".

In fact quite the reverse, in a really close relationship with someone we tend *not* to notice their physical appearance. Most of the time we only really look at them when asked to. We can get so used to living with a person that it can give us quite a jolt to really see them sometimes and realise that they are ageing!

Much the same thing happens in our relationships with the animals who share our daily lives. We see them but do not see them, or maybe we see them more truly when we look beyond the physical body. Looking back down the decades to the small girl who loved a special little dog as a brother I realise that I have not changed so much. I am quite surprised now and then to discover that the little people who share my home and my daily life are actually cats and dogs!

This is not at all the same thing as deliberately turning our pets into substitute children to fulfil our own emotional needs; on the contrary it means accepting our pets for the individual and special personalities that they are, and loving them for being themselves. Only now, as we approach the closing years of the twentieth century is the world at large, and science in particular, coming to an acceptance of what animal lovers have known for hundreds of years. Animals are *good* for people!

Once firmly banned from all caring institutions animals are now not only welcome as visitors but are actually paid staff members in many instances. It has been found that dogs, cats and birds in geriatric and psychiatric institutions not only help to keep the patients relaxed but often stimulate them into taking an interest in life again. The companionship of animals often has a remarkable effect on those of any age, but teenagers in particular, who have fallen foul of the law. Particularly if they are given responsibility for their welfare.

It has been proved that patients undergoing serious heart surgery stand a far better chance of making a good recovery if they return home to a much loved pet. Possibly the knowledge that another living creature is dependant upon them also (if only subconsciously) gives a much-needed boost to the patient's all important will to live. It has been proven scientifically that our blood pressure actually drops and our heart rate slows when we rest our hand on the head of a beloved dog or take a special cat into our lap.

This is something that pet-lovers have always known; who among us has not felt a lightening of the spirit on being greeted by a loved and loving dog at the end of a work-wearying day? What cat-lover has not felt tension and fatigue drop away when their little friend settles in their lap, its throbbing purr singing its own relaxation and contentment to the world? Our small friends give us so much, more I sometimes think than we can ever return in full measure.

Most of us do our best; we provide warmth, shelter, food and medical care, but we fail, I sometimes feel in less tangible ways. Our lives are so full, so busy, that we do not always find the time to give our dog or cat the understanding and companionship that it, like every other living creature needs. If we could change places with our pet, just for a day, we would probably be quite shocked to discover how lonely it could be if one were the *only* non-human creature in the household. Especially if those humans had little time in the frantic comings and goings of their own lives to communicate beyond basic calls to meals and bed!

Yet this is the sort of life we often expect our cat or dog to lead. It is really quite amazing that there are so few really delinquent dogs, and even fewer cats getting themselves and their owners into trouble with anti-social behaviour!

The old adage about Satan finding mischief for idle hands (or paws) to do is as true for dogs as it is for children. It is the lonely and bored dog who tears things up, digs holes and is generally destructive around the place.

Maybe a good rule of thumb should be not to have one animal if you cannot have two. Surprisingly cats and dogs, traditionally arch enemies, often become very good friends indeed when they are the only four-legged people in a family.

Having siblings from the same litter is often a good idea with kittens. Two kittens are usually half the trouble of one as they amuse each other. The same cannot usually be said however of puppies. Two puppies may be about four times as much trouble as one as, like children, they seem to egg one another on and think up mischief that one alone would not. It is a good plan to have a second dog when one is middle-aged (this often stops the older one getting too staid too soon), and repeating this a few years later by getting a new puppy after the old one has died. In this way the home is never left totally bereft of canine company and the dogs themselves always have another of their own species for company.

If we are often guilty of giving too little to our pets they in turn are not, in fact most companion animals live up wonderfully to the role in life we have designated them. Above all they give generously and uncritically of their love and devotion. No wonder most of us feel so much better in the company of a pet; this sort of love is not so easy to come by. I once heard a person who had to deal all the time with those saddest of creatures, abandoned dogs ask; How could people? Throwing away a dog is throwing away love and who can afford to do that!

While dogs like the incomparable Nana in *Peter Pan* may not be too common, nevertheless children who grow up where a loving and loved dog is a respected member of the family not only are the recipients of this wonderful unconditional love but learn so many lessons along the way about kindness, patience, tolerance, responsibility and enjoyment of life that they cannot help but grow into a better person in every way, including their dealings with other humans. Even if our own family pet does fall far short of being a Nana we can still recognise the importance of the part they play in the family as friend and mentor.

Looking back over many years of living with dogs and cats I sometimes think that most of the *really* important lessons I have learned over the years have been from these small people in animal bodies; lessons about living, and loving - and losing. And the most important lesson of all, being there, in the minute, while it is all happening.

We talk about our dogs and our cats; and at times are tempted to believe that we do own them. By the laws of this world we do, we may have paid out hard cash for them, we support them, and we pay their licence fees; we are also responsible for their behaviour. We are also responsible in much the same way for our children. But we do not own them even though we call them our children. There is a wise old proverb that says 'Our children are not given but lent'. We are privileged to share time in our joint lives together. So with our animal friends. While their lives and ours run together we are all part of the same family unit, by acknowledging this we will all be winners.

Chapter Twelve

Happy Endings

Brothers and sisters I bid you beware
Of giving your heart to a dog to tear.

Rudyard Kipling

The Power of the Dog

The average lifespan of a dog or a cat is approximately one sixth that of our own. To many people this is a big minus, but it can also be seen as a plus; for in our longer lives, compared with theirs, we have time in our life to enjoy the close company of so many four-footed friends. Each bringing with it not only its own personality but its own special blend of happiness and tears, (usually much more of the former) to enrich our lives and help us, in their own small way, to grow in stature and wisdom.

Endings are always traumatic, and nonetheless so than when the inevitable passage of time claims an old friend. A decade or more of love and companionship deserves to be repaid with a parting as pain-free and happy as possible.

Whether or not we deserve to be looked up to as a God by our pets is very debatable, nevertheless the fact remains that we *do* have an omnipotent power over their lives. Even the power of Life and Death. We can give them away, sell them, abandon them or have their life snuffed out if they displease us. We may do the decent thing and take it to the local vet to be humanely put down or we can shoot it ourselves in our own back yard. Whatever we do we will not be tried for murder.

Few people would actually sell their pet. Animals that are sold are usually those who are being bred for profit, and that is not what this book is all about. We would only give it away if circumstances were such that we had little alternative and then we would endeavour to ensure that it was going to a good home, and if you are reading this book at all it is most unlikely that you are the sort of person who would take their cat or dog out and simply abandon it to its fate in a hostile world; but with the best of intentions we do not always do the best we can when the inevitable parting comes.

The best that most people think they can do is to take it to the vet and have it put to sleep, a euphemistic phrase we like to use to make ourselves feel better about the whole thing. We are *not* taking it to be put to sleep, from *this* sleep there is no awakening, we are taking it to the vet to be put to death. We, as humans, suffer from a curious malaise, the inability to accept death as a fact of life. Everything *must* die, it is the price we pay for living.

We reveal our inability to come to grips with death in our language. Our relatives and friends pass over or pass on, when looking ahead to beyond our own demise we usually say something like; if anything happens to me... Our pets are put to sleep and, with what really seems like incredible carelessness, we lose both people and pets!

Modern Science has given us the power to extend and prolong life, but with this ability we seem to have lost much of our belief in a life after the death of the physical body.

It is probably the combination of these two factors that make it so hard for us to accept the inevitable truth that for everything under the sun there is a time to be born and a time to die. Sometimes we can show our love most by accepting this instead of fighting it.

Many years ago, when I was at my Convent Boarding School one of the prayers we rattled off cheerfully (and for the most part thoughtlessly) to God and the Sister in charge in the dormitory each night was the prayer for a happy death.

Those of my relatives who were not of a religious bent considered this extremely morbid. I did not, for a happy death conjured up in my imagination a bedside party to wish me farewell before I was escorted by my Guardian Angel to the next world!

The crucial factor in this scenario was, of course, the fact that I was at home, surrounded by all the things and people I knew and loved. It is *this* sort of happy ending I think we should accord to our much-loved four-footed family members when the inevitable time of parting comes.

It is not of course always possible. There are times when, with the best will in the world, our pet dies in the animal hospital or the vet's surgery. But there are equally many times when we can avoid this.

We often *know* in our innermost heart, that a beloved cat or dog is dying and that no amount of modern medical skill is going to save it. And we still, battening down the still small voice, assuring ourselves we are doing our best, take it to the veterinarian where, defying science, it dies, alone, and probably afraid, worst of all feeling we have deserted it, our own pain is then so much the greater than if we could have been there with it to say a last, loving Goodbye.

A friend of mine once took a much-loved cat who had a recurring skin cancer into the vet. She went into the surgery with no thought of having it put to sleep. By some ghastly failure in communication the vet apparently thought that was what she wanted. My friend told me that even when he put the needle in her cat's vein she did not realise what was happening. When she told me about it afterwards she kept saying; "I did not even have a chance to say Goodbye - I feel so dreadful!".

We all need a chance to say goodbye. My life has been shared with so many animals that inevitably the partings have been many; and I know that those that have caused me most grief have been the ones when I did not have that chance.

The worst of all are the times when a dearly loved animal friend simply disappears without trace. The hoping, without real hope, is truly the most painful parting of all.

Of the many cats I have loved down the years Tabitha will always stand out as special. Not only did I think this about her but she did too! Curiously enough on my first meeting with her I thought she was one of the plainest kittens I had ever seen. She was blotched, mottled and striped in two shades of grey, she had ears like a bat and a long stringy tail. Her mother was a beautiful Tonkinese and from her she inherited an extremely loud Siamese voice, and probably a good deal of her personality and intelligence and her firm belief that she was *not* as other cats!

As time went on I began to consider her extraordinarily beautiful, her loud voice was music to me, in spite of the many awful misdeeds she committed in the course of her life I came round to her way of thinking, she *was* superior to all other cats!

Superior she may have been, but not in virtue. She teased and bullied unmercifully the ordinary cats she lived with. She caught, killed - and ate my beloved budgie and she was prone to disappear on rabbit hunting safaris for days at a time, leaving me in a state of angst about her. She would return home days later, usually around 2 am, announcing her presence by climbing the flyscreen at my bedroom window and bawling for admittance at the very top of her considerable voice, as she hung there, claws firmly embedded in the mesh, till she heard me roll out of bed and head for the front door. By the time I opened it she was waiting for me and hurtled past me with rapturous shouts of joy.

She was always ensconced in bed by the time I crawled back in and I would drop back to sleep with her contented purr thrumming in my ears, happy and relieved that she was safe home and firmly stifling the temptation to speculate on the number of fleas she might have brought home with her!

Her longest trip away from home was ten days so I was not specially worried when I went to bed on the third night of what was to be her final trip. That night I dreamed of her; one of those specially vivid dreams that remain in the memory for ever. Ten years later it is as clear as the morning after. I dreamed that Tabitha was walking towards me across the kitchen floor; her tail perpendicular in greeting just as I had seen her so many times; she seemed to be bathed in a soft golden light that had no visible source and she said to me (I do not think she actually spoke the words but rather they were transmitted directly from her mind to mine) "Don't worry about me; I'm all right!". She then seemed to just fade away into the light and I woke up.

My first words on waking were "Tabitha is dead; we shall never see her again!". My husband told me I was being pessimistic; she had often been away longer than this; she would be back, yelling for admittance in her usual arrogant way. His words failed to convince me. I *knew* she was dead and that somehow her indestructible little spirit had communicated to me through the medium of the dream state. I was right; I never did see my much loved cat again; but the memory of that dream has stayed with me down the years and given me consolation when I have had to face the death of other much loved animal friends.

The strange business of Minnie and the rumpled bed was another instance that led to my conviction that our pets are no more snuffed out at death than we are. Minnie was a portly little Fox Terrier and one of the most enchanting and lovable characters I have ever known. She was also a very determined little person and she and I had an on-going difference of opinion over her making a comfortable nest for herself on my bed when she was very tired, or very muddy, or both. She would get into the room when no-one was around, work up the covers with her often dirty little paws until she had a cosy nest just to her liking, and settle down for, she considered, a well-earned rest after a hard day digging at rabbit holes. If I did not actually catch her there she usually left ample signs of occupation!

A few days after Minnie died I went into my room and found the bed covers pulled up in the distinctive way that was Minnie's trademark. I stopped in my tracks, my mouth opening to admonish her; then I remembered, Minnie was dead. There was only one explanation, one of the other dogs or cats must be responsible.

A few days later the same thing happened. My husband was the first to discover the nest this time. Looks as if someone else has inherited Minnies favourite place! he commented. I agreed, like him I wanted to find a rational explanation for something that appeared quite irrational.

A week later the whole family went out for the day. Before we left I made the bed with care, taking pains to leave the quilt quite smooth. My husband followed me out of the room, closing the door firmly behind him. We checked that all the cats were outside, locked the half-grown dog in the stables and put the other in the car before we closed and locked the door behind us.

When we drove home several hours later all four cats were waiting on the doorstep for us; My husband went to let the dog out of the stables while I unlocked the door. I went straight to my bedroom; I flung open the door to throw my handbag on the bed and kick off my shoes; I did neither, but stopped, frozen, in the doorway. This was one of the very few times in my life when I literally felt the hair on the back of my neck prickle; I called the rest of the family who crowded behind me in the doorway in a sort of stunned silence before we all began to speak at once. The bedclothes were pulled up into such a thorough and deep nest that I almost expected to see her shameless little face and button-bright eyes looking at me over the covers and was quite relieved to see that there were no muddy paw-marks all over everything! We never had any evidence again that Minnie was still around; there was no need; she had made her point.

Cindy was a big red dog, a Red Setter cross Labrador, she was my dear friend and loving companion for fifteen years. Finally the day came when I knew we must part, her life had become a burden, not a pleasure any more. One of the greatest pleasures in her life had been to ride in the car with me, she would sit up in the very centre of the back seat taking a great interest in everything. When I looked in the rear vision mirror I could see her face. On this last day I took her a ride in the car; I had to help her climb in, but her tail wagged for me, she was too tired to sit up as she used to, but when I glanced round at her she seemed to be enjoying the ride. I drove to the vets surgery and left her in the car, I asked him to come out to my car and humanely put down a very old dog. Her dim old eyes were on my face and her tail gave a reassuring wag, I stroked her silky head as the lethal needle found her vein. With a sigh, she was gone.

I drove home with her and she was buried with love in our garden. Cindy had been one of my closest canine companions for a very long time; we had many, many happy times together. I loved her dearly but I did not grieve for her as I have for many other animals who have died for I knew that, as far as I possibly could, I had given her a happy ending and by doing so I had in some small measure managed to repay a little of the boundless love she had given me over the years. Because we have such a phobia, as humans, about facing up to the reality of death we often think we will make things easier for ourselves when the inevitable time of parting draws close if we hand our pet over to the vet; ask for it to be Put To Sleep and walk out of the surgery. Believe you me, you are not!

Sooner or later you must accept the fact that your much loved pet is *not* asleep; it is dead, and when you do, and it is too late to do anything about it, that you were not there with it in these last moments.

There is a saying attributed to that great author, Anonymous, which goes something like this:

"The end is something that proves everything, and in much the same vein Longfellow wrote: Great is the art of beginning but greater is the art of ending."

Inevitably, because our small friends have shorter lives than we do, we can expect many times to have to face the loss of a loved pet. There are two common reactions, either to rush out and acquire another immediately or to say; "I will *never* have another dog - or cat; it is too heart-breaking when they die".

As in so many situations in life neither the right nor the left is the way to go but to choose the middle path.

It is heart-breaking to lose a much loved animal so give yourself time to grieve but time *does* heal. If you go out too soon to replace a pet, that is just what it will be, a replacement, not an entity in its own right. You will forever expect it to be just like the dear departed, and this of course it cannot be, for animals, just like people, are distinct personalities.

Give yourself time, and when you feel ready, then start looking for another friend, not as a replacement but for itself. It is an odd thing but far more often than I have gone looking some creature in desperate need of a home and friendship has found me at such times!

If you take the extreme view that you will never, ever, have another pet, and of course it is your right to do this if you wish, then you will be denying yourself a chance of another rich and rewarding relationship. And what better memorial could your dead pet have than another happy much loved pet? Every ending, however painful, brings with it the promise of a new beginning.

FREE DETAILED CATALOGUE

A detailed illustrated catalogue is available on request, SAE or International Postal Coupon appreciated. Titles are available direct from Capall Bann, post free in the UK (cheque or PO with order) or from good bookshops and specialist outlets. Title currently available include:

Animals, Mind Body Spirit & Folklore
Angels and Goddesses - Celtic Christianity & Paganism by Michael Howard
Arthur - The Legend Unveiled by C Johnson & E Lung
Auguries and Omens - The Magical Lore of Birds by Yvonne Aburrow
Book of the Veil The by Peter Paddon
Call of the Horned Piper by Nigel Jackson
Cats' Company by Ann Walker
Celtic Lore & Druidic Ritual by Rhiannon Ryall
Compleat Vampyre - The Vampyre Shaman: Werewolves & Witchery by Nigel Jackson
Crystal Clear - A Guide to Quartz Crystal by Jennifer Dent
Earth Dance - A Year of Pagan Rituals by Jan Brodie

Earth Magic by Margaret McArthur
Enchanted Forest - The Magical Lore of Trees by Yvonne Aburrow
Healing Homes by Jennifer Dent
Herbcraft - Shamanic & Ritual Use of Herbs by Susan Lavender & Anna Franklin
In Search of Herne the Hunter by Eric Fitch
Inner Space Workbook - Developing Counselling & Magical Skills Through the Tarot
Kecks, Keddles & Kesh by Michael Bayley
Living Tarot by Ann Walker
Magical Incenses and Perfumes by Jan Brodie
Magical Lore of Animals by Yvonne Aburrow
Magical Lore of Cats by Marion Davies

Magical Lore of Herbs by Marion Davies
Masks of Misrule - The Horned God & His Cult in Europe by Nigel Jackson
Mysteries of the Runes by Michael Howard
Oracle of Geomancy by Nigel Pennick
Patchwork of Magic by Julia Day
Pathworking - A Practical Book of Guided Meditations by Pete Jennings
Pickingill Papers - The Origins of Gardnerian Wicca by Michael Howard
Psychic Animals by Dennis Bardens
Psychic Self Defence - Real Solutions by Jan Brodie
Runic Astrology by Nigel Pennick
Sacred Animals by Gordon MacLellan
Sacred Grove - The Mysteries of the Forest by Yvonne Aburrow
Sacred Geometry by Nigel Pennick
Sacred Lore of Horses The by Marion Davies
Sacred Ring - Pagan Origins British Folk Festivals & Customs by Michael Howard
Secret Places of the Goddess by Philip Heselton
Talking to the Earth by Gordon Maclellan
Taming the Wolf - Full Moon Meditations by Steve Hounsome
The Goddess Year by Nigel Pennick & Helen Field
West Country Wicca by Rhiannon Ryall
Witches of Oz The by Matthew & Julia Phillips

Capall Bann is owned and run by people actively involved in many of the areas in which we publish. Our list is expanding rapidly so do contact us for details on the latest releases. We guarantee our mailing list will never be released to other companies or organisations.

Capall Bann Publishing, Freshfields, Chieveley, Berks, RG20 8TF